Developing Hybrid Applications for the iPhone

Developing Hybrid Applications for the iPhone

Using HTML, CSS, and JavaScript to Build Dynamic Apps for the iPhone

Lee S. Barney

Addison-Wesley

Upper Saddle River, NJ • Boston • Indianapolis • San Francisco
New York • Toronto • Montreal • London • Munich • Paris • Madrid
Cape Town • Sydney • Tokyo • Singapore • Mexico City

The publisher offers excellent discounts on this book when ordered in quantity for bulk purchases or special sales, which may include electronic versions and/or custom covers and content particular to your business, training goals, marketing focus, and branding interests. For more information, please contact:

U.S. Corporate and Government Sales
(800) 382-3419
corpsales@pearsontechgroup.com

For sales outside the United States, please contact:

International Sales
international@pearson.com

Visit us on the Web: informit.com/aw

Library of Congress Cataloging-in-Publication Data

Barney, Lee.
Developing hybrid applications for the iPhone : using HTML, CSS, and JavaScript to build dynamic apps for the iPhone / Lee S. Barney.

p. cm.

Includes index.

ISBN 978-0-321-60416-3 (pbk. : alk. paper) 1. iPhone (Smartphone)–Programming. 2. Application software–Development. 3. Cross-platform software development. I. Title.

TK6570.M6B37 2009

621.3845'6–dc22

2009019162

ISBN-13: 978-0-321-60416-3
ISBN-10: 0-321-60416-4

Text printed in the United States on recycled paper at R.R. Donnelley in Crawfordsville, Indiana.

First printing June 2009

Editor-in-Chief
Karen Gettman

Acquisitions Editor
Chuck Toporek

Development Editor
Sheri Cain

Managing Editor
Kristy Hart

Project Editor
Jovana San Nicolas-Shirley

Copy Editor
Deadline Driven Publishing

Indexer
Erika Millen

Proofreader
Kathy Ruiz

Technical Reviewers
August Trometer
Randall Tamura

Publishing Coordinator
Romny French

Cover Designer
Gary Adair

Compositor
Jake McFarland

❖

This book is dedicated to my wonderful wife Joan
and our five boys who have put up with me
being too busy while this book was being created.
Eternity isn't long enough to be with you.

❖

Table of Contents

Preface xiii

1 Developing with Dashcode and Xcode 1

Section 1: Using Dashcode and the Custom QuickConnect Template 1

Section 2: Using Xcode and the Custom QuickConnect Template 4

Section 3: Using Xcode and the Custom PhoneGap Template 9

Section 4: Introduction to Basic Objective-C 11

Section 5: Objective-C QuickConnectiPhone Application Structure 14

Section 6: Objective-C PhoneGap Application Structure 17

Section 7: Embedding Web Content: QuickConnectiPhone 19

Section 8: Embedding Web Content: PhoneGap 23

Summary 24

2 JavaScript Modularity and iPhone Applications 25

Section 1: Modularity 25

Section 2: The QuickConnect JavaScript Framework—A Modularity Example 26

Section 3: The QuickConnectiPhone Implementation of the Modular Design 34

Section 4: Business and View Application Controller Implementations 38

Section 5: Error Application Controller Implementation 42

Section 6: Application Functionality Creation Steps 43

Summary 43

3 Creating iPhone User Interfaces 45

Section 1: Apple's Human Interface Guide 45

Section 2: List- and Browser-Based Interfaces 48

Section 3: Nonlist-Based View Applications 51

Section 4: Immersion Applications 55
Section 5: Creating and Using Custom CSS Transforms 57
Section 6: Using and Creating a Drag-and-Drop/Scale/Rotate Module 64
Summary 74

4 GPS, Acceleration, and Other Native Functions with QuickConnect 75
Section 1: JavaScript Device Activation 75
Section 2: Objective-C Device Activation 81
Section 3: Objective-C Implementation of the QuickConnectiPhone Architecture 88
Summary 94

5 Hybrid Applications, GPS, Acceleration, and Other Native Functions with PhoneGap 95
Section 1: JavaScript Device Activation 95
Section 2: Objective-C Device Activation 102
Summary 109

6 Embedding Google Maps 111
Section 1: Displaying a Map from Within Your QuickConnect JavaScript Application 111
Section 2: Objective-C Implementation of the QuickConnect Mapping Module 115
Summary 126

7 Database Access 127
Section 1: BrowserDBAccess Example Application 127
Section 2: Using WebView SQLite Databases 129
Section 3: Using Native SQLite Databases 133
Section 4: Using the DataAccessObject with WebKit Engine Databases 135
Section 5: Using the DataAccessObject with Native Databases 145
Summary 154

8 Remote Data Access 155

Section 1: BrowserAJAXAccess Example Application 155

Section 2: Using the ServerAccessObject 157

Section 3: ServerAccessObject 162

Section 4: Security Control Functions 171

Summary 172

A Introduction to JSON 173

Section 1: Background 173

Section 2: A JSON JavaScript API 175

Summary 178

B The QuickConnectFamily Development Roadmap 179

C The PhoneGap Development Roadmap 183

Preface

This book shows you how to create a new type of iPhone application: hybrid applications written in HTML, CSS, and JavaScript. Hybrid iPhone applications are standalone applications that run like regular applications on your iPhone, but don't require the files to live on a server on the Internet.

Creating hybrid iPhone applications reduces creation time and the learning curve required to get your application into the hands of your customers, because you don't have to learn Objective-C or have an intimate knowledge of the Cocoa frameworks.

Hybrid Application Development Tools

This book covers the two most commonly used open-source JavaScript software packages for writing applications for the iPhone and iPod touch devices: QuickConnectiPhone and PhoneGap. These packages enable you to build applications that access native device features directly from JavaScript, such as vibration, GPS location information, the accelerometer, and many other things—all without writing a single line of Objective-C or Cocoa.

QuickConnectiPhone, downloaded from http://sourceforge.net/projects/quickconnect, exposes the most native device behavior and provides a highly engineered, full-featured framework for development use. QuickConnectiPhone dramatically reduces your application's time-to-market because part of the framework consists of all of the glue code you have to typically write in Objective-C, Cocoa, and JavaScript. Best of all, it does not require a remote server for hosting JavaScript, HTML, and CSS files.

The second package is PhoneGap, downloaded from http://phonegap.com. PhoneGap exposes fewer native behaviors and is a library rather than a full-fledged framework. As a library, PhoneGap enables you to engineer your application any way you want. It does, however, require a remote server for hosting files.

To reduce the learning curve and improve your understanding, good, solid examples are used throughout this book.

If you want to create installable iPhone applications, have the web skills required, and want to create dynamic, compelling solutions that people will use, this book shows you how using these two packages.

Table P.1 compares what each package can do at the time of writing this book.

Table P.1 **Comparing the Features of QuickConnectiPhone and PhoneGap**

Behavior/Data Available	QuickConnectiPhone	PhoneGap
GPS	Yes	Yes
Accelerometer	Yes	Yes
Vibrate	Yes	Yes
System sounds	Yes	Yes
Ad-hoc (Bonjour) networking	Yes	No
Sync cable networking	Yes	No
Browser-based database access	Yes	No
Shipped database access	Yes	No
Drag-and-drop library	Yes	No
AJAX wrapper	Yes	No
Record/Play audio files	Yes	No
Embedded Google maps	Yes	No
Charts and graphs library	Yes	No

How to Use This Book

Each chapter is organized into two parts. The first part shows you how to use the relevant feature of either QuickConnectiPhone or PhoneGap to accomplish a particular task, such as getting the current geolocation of the device. The second part of the chapter shows how the code behind the JavaScript call is written and how it works. You can decide how deep into the JavaScript and Objective-C you want to delve.

The book is organized as follows:

- Chapter 1, "Developing with Dashcode and Xcode," teaches you how to use Dashcode and Xcode together with QuickConnectiPhone and PhoneGap to quickly create fun-to-use applications that run on the iPhone. This chapter includes basic Dashcode use and methods for moving your Dashcode application into Xcode for compiling and running on devices.
- Chapter 2, "JavaScript Modularity and iPhone Applications," teaches you how to dramatically reduce your time to market by taking advantage of the modularity of the QuickConnectiPhone framework. How front controllers, application controllers, and JavaScript reflection are used in code is explained.
- Chapter 3, "Creating iPhone User Interfaces," helps ensure that Apple App Store distribution approves your applications. It describes best practices for creating highly usable iPhone applications. The different types of applications usually created for iPhones are described as well as pitfalls to watch out for.
- Chapter 4, "GPS, Acceleration, and Other Native Functions with QuickConnectiPhone," shows you how to get GPS, acceleration, and device

description information, and it teaches you how to vibrate your phone and play and record audio files. You use the QuickConnectiPhone framework to access and use these device behaviors. These abilities give your applications a truly native, fun feel.

- Chapter 5, "GPS, Acceleration, and Other Native Functions with PhoneGap," shows you how to get GPS, acceleration, and device description information as well as how to vibrate your phone and play and record audio files. You use the PhoneGap library to access and use these native device behaviors. These abilities give your applications a truly native, fun feel.
- Chapter 6, "Embedding Google Maps," shows you how to put a Google map inside your application using QuickConnectiPhone. This is one of the most requested pieces of functionality and means you won't have to send your users to the map application!
- Chapter 7, "Database Access," shows you how to get information from and store data in SQLite databases included in your application created with the QuickConnectiPhone framework. Do you need to ship a predefined set of data in a database with your new applications? Read this chapter.
- Chapter 8, "Remote Data Access," shows you how to make accessing and using data from remote servers and/or service in your installed application easy with a wrapper that lets you pull information from anywhere. Maybe you need to get data from an online blog and merge it with a Twitter feed. QuickConnectiPhone's remote-data-access module makes it easy.

The following appendices are also included:

- Appendix A, "Introduction to JSON," provides you with a brief introduction to JavaScript Object Notation (JSON). JSON is one of the most commonly used and easiest ways to transfer your data wherever it needs to go.
- Appendix B, "The QuickConnectFamily Development Roadmap," provides an overview of the growth of QuickConnectiPhone in the future. If you plan to create applications for iPhones and other platforms, such as Google's Android phones, Nokia phones, Blackberries, and desktops such as Mac OS X, Linux, and Windows, you should take a look at this appendix.
- Appendix C, "The PhoneGap Development Roadmap," provides an overview of the growth of PhoneGap in the future. If you plan to create applications for iPhones and other platforms, such as Google's Android phones, Nokia phones, Blackberries, and desktops such as Mac OS X, Linux, and Windows, you should take a look at this appendix.

Online Resources

QuickConnectiPhone and PhoneGap are undergoing rapid development. To keep up with the new functions and capabilities and to learn more, use the following links.

QuickConnectiPhone

- Download examples and the framework from https://sourceforge.net/projects/quickconnect/
- Review the development blog at http://tetontech.wordpress.com
- Read the Wiki at http://quickconnect.pbwiki.com/FrontPage
- Find the Google group at http://groups.google.com/group/quickconnectiPhone/
- Twitter at http://twitter.com/quickconnect

PhoneGap

- Download examples and the framework from https://sourceforge.net/projects/phonegapinstall/
- Visit the web site at http://www.phonegap.com/
- Read the Wiki at http://phonegap.pbwiki.com/
- Find the Google group at http://groups.google.com/group/phonegap
- Twitter at http://twitter.com/phonegap

Prerequisites

You need a basic understanding of HTML, CSS, and JavaScript to effectively use this book. If you have created web pages using these tools, you are well on your way to creating iPhone applications. If you need help with Objecive-C in both QuickConnectiPhone and PhoneGap, it is provided. This book is not intended to be an introductory book on Objective-C or how to use it to develop iPhone applications.

You need to download and install Apple's Xcode tools from the iPhone developer web site at http://developer.apple.com/iphone. This requires Mac OS X 10.5 or greater and an Intel-based Mac.

Although it isn't required, you should also have either an iPhone or an iPod touch, so you can test and run the applications on those devices.

Acknowledgments

A special thanks to Daniel Barney for working through and debugging the embedded Google maps code. Thanks also to my coworkers in the Brigham Young University–Idaho Computer Information Technology Department for listening and giving suggestions.

About the Author

Lee S. Barney (Rexburg, Idaho) is a professor at Brigham Young University–Idaho in the Computer Information Technology Department of the Business and Communication College. He has worked as CIO and CTO of @HomeSoftware, a company that produced web-based, mobile data, and scheduling applications for the home health care industry. Prior to this, he worked for more than seven years as a programmer, senior software engineer, quality assurance manager, development manager, and project manager for AutoSimulations, Inc., the leading supplier of planning and scheduling software to the semiconductor industry. He is the author of *Oracle Database AJAX & PHP Web Application Development*.

Contacting the Author

To contact the author by email, use quickconnectfamily@gmail.com. For other types of contact, use Twitter, the Wiki, and Google Group links provided earlier.

1

Developing with Dashcode and Xcode

When used together, Dashcode and Xcode provide the power and ease of use needed to create unique, exciting, hybrid iPhone applications. Because both of these tools were extended with custom templates for hybrid iPhone applications, you do not have to "roll your own" Objective-C wrapper. In the first three sections, you learn how to use existing hybrid iPhone application templates for Dashcode and Xcode. Using these templates lets you quickly create hybrid iPhone applications. A short discussion of basic Objective-C and how an Objective-C iPhone application is structured in the two most heavily used hybrid application tools—QuickConnectiPhone and PhoneGap—is also included in Sections 4 through 8.

Section 1: Using Dashcode and the Custom QuickConnect Template

Because much of the user interface and interaction for iPhone hybrid applications are created using HTML, JavaScript, and CSS, Dashcode is where you do most of your development and debugging. Dashcode's drag-and-drop interface builder is unique in its scope and ease of use. Dashcode is used to create most of the application, and it also used to debug it using the simulator and built-in debugging tools.

Because most of the code for iPhone hybrid applications is similar, the creation of a template containing the common code would prevent the need to rewrite or import it each time a new project is started. For a discussion of common code, see Chapter 2, "JavaScript Modularity and iPhone Applications."

The QuickConnectiPhone download is available from http://sourceforge.net/projects/quickconnect and it includes a Dashcode template to assist you in creating hybrid iPhone applications. The QuickConnectFamily installer inserts this template into Dashcode. Unfortunately, at the time of the writing of this book, the creators of the alternative, PhoneGap, do not provide a Dashcode template.

After you run the QuickConnectFamily installer and launch Dashcode, you can find the QuickConnectiPhone template at the bottom of the Dashboard Widget template selection dialog. Double-clicking the QuickConnectiPhone icon takes you directly into the main Dashcode screen. The blank user interface displays on the screen. Figure 1.1 illustrates what the running Dashcode application looks like.

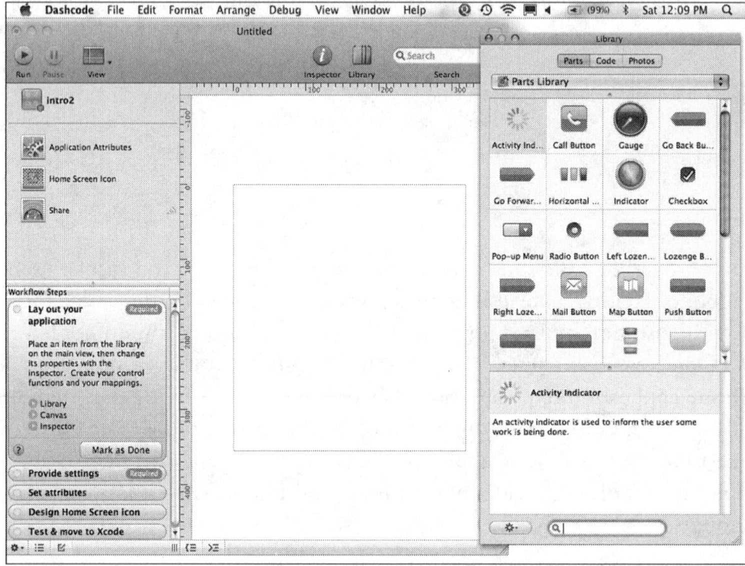

Figure 1.1 The QuickConnectiPhone template is used in Dashcode. The standard Library dialog is displayed.

To understand and easily use the files included in the framework, you must first create a simple user interface using Dashcode and deploy it to your iPhone using Xcode. The user interface created here consists of only a button and a text field. When the button is clicked, the text field displays "You did it!"

Hybrid Applications and the Alert Dialog

People accustomed to writing in JavaScript often use the Alert dialog to debug an application or notify the user of a piece of information. The `alert` function in JavaScript is actually a call into the containing browser's native code rather than something that the JavaScript engine handles.

This is not implemented in QuickConnectiPhone applications because the use of dialogs violates the iPhone user interface standards Apple provided. For debugging, you can use the Dashcode debugger. If you move your application to Xcode you can use the `debug` function to display messages in the Xcode console.

> PhoneGap does provide Alert dialog functionality, but it does not provide the Xcode debug function.
>
> To notify users of important pieces of information, insert them into an HTML div or another element regardless of which tool you use.
>
> Remember, be alert, don't alert.

To create this user interface, be sure the Library dialog is open. If it is not, click the Library icon on the top bar of Dashcode. Then, find the Text part at the bottom of the parts library and drag it on to the blank application screen. A new text area displays at the top of your application's interface and contains the word Text. This text, by default, has a width of 100 percent. Dashcode has dynamically inserted an HTML div tag into the underlying index.html file of your application and some JavaScript to fill it with whatever text, background colors, and so on that you choose.

For this example, you change the id of the text div to `display` and empty the text field. This is done using the interface entity inspector. Selecting the Inspector icon in the top bar of Dashcode activates this dialog. Select the red and white tab in the upper-left hand corner of the Inspector, change the ID field to read `display`, and then clear the Label field.

Add a Push button to the interface by dragging and dropping it outside the text field. The inspector now displays the information for the button instead of the text field. Select the blue cube in the upper right-hand corner of the Inspector dialog. This causes the Behaviors tab to appear. This tab enables you to define JavaScript functions as handlers for any of the user interface types of events listed. Notice that many of the standard JavaScript mouse events are not seen. They have been replaced with `ongesturestart`, `ongesturechange`, and `ongestureend`. Enter `changeText` in the handler section of the `onclick` event. This inserts a `changeText` function in the main.js file, displays it to you, and enables you to define what should happen when the `onclick` event is fired. In this simple case, place the following code in the `changeText` function:

```
document.getElementById('display').innerHTML = 'You did it!';
```

The sample application is now ready to run in the iPhone simulator. Select the Run icon in the upper left-hand corner of Dashcode. This launches the simulator and runs your application in it. Figure 1.2 shows the simple example application running in the simulator.

Having completed and debugged the creation of the application, you can now move the code into Xcode for deployment as an installable application.

To start, you use Dashcode to deploy the current application. If you do not, the code is hidden inside your Dashcode project and has directives in it that only Dashcode can understand. Click the Share icon in the left-hand section of Dashcode to show the deployment screen. This enables you to save the completed HTML, CSS, and JavaScript to disk in a form that is ready to embed in your application. Enter a name for a new directory in the Path field to create a directory on the hard drive of your machine. The files are then

Figure 1.2 The simple example application runs in the Dashcode simulator after the button is clicked.

stored in this new directory. They are also ready to be imported into Xcode. Figure 1.3 shows the deployment screen.

For more information about the JavaScript files included in this template and how to use them to make application creation easier, see Chapter 2.

Section 2: Using Xcode and the Custom QuickConnect Template

Because you ran the QuickConnectFamily installer, the Xcode QuickConnectiPhone Application template has been installed for you. Use it to create the Xcode project for your QuickConnectiPhone hybrid application. This section walks you through how this is done. The QuickConnectFamily wiki includes a video of this same process (http://quickconnect.pbwiki.com/Moving-Dashcode-projects-to-Xcode).

To do this, select New → Project. Select iPhone OS Applications and the QuickConnect iPhone Application icon displays. Double-click the icon, name your project, and then select or create a directory to locate it in on your hard drive. Xcode creates a project that includes the Objective-C files needed to run your JavaScript application directly on the

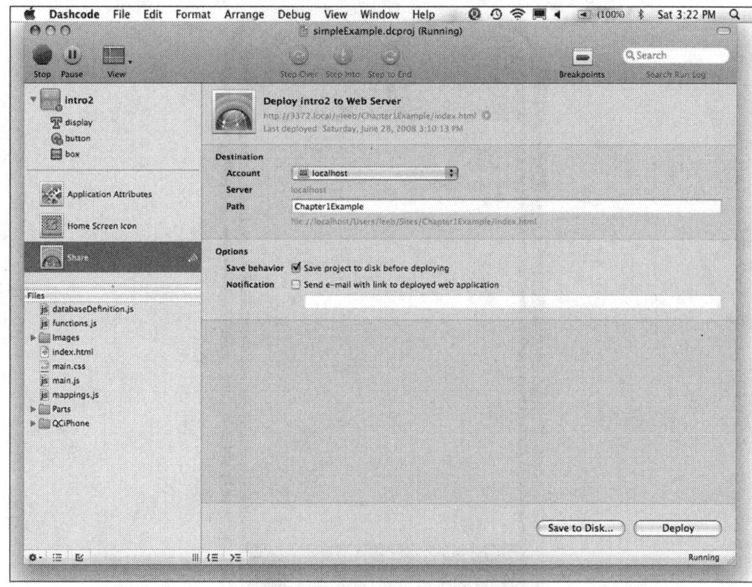

Figure 1.3 The deployment screen shows the completed application being deployed to the Chapter1Example web server directory.

device without network or Internet access. In the Resources group of your application are a series of HTML, CSS, and JavaScript placeholder files.

One of these placeholder files is index.html. It contains the HTML, CSS, and JavaScript for an example application that is ready to run. Figure 1.4 shows this example running on the simulator as an installed application.

To include the files created previously in Dashcode in this project, delete the following files:

- index.html
- main.css
- main.js
- Files in the Parts group
- Files in the Images group

After removing these files, import the index.html, main.css, and main.js files. Do this by right-control clicking the Resources group, and selecting Add → Existing Files. Browse to the directory that you deployed your Dashcode application to and select index.html, main.css, and main.js. You can copy the files into the Xcode project or use them where they currently are. For this example, select the Copy items into destination group's folder checkbox each time you are asked.

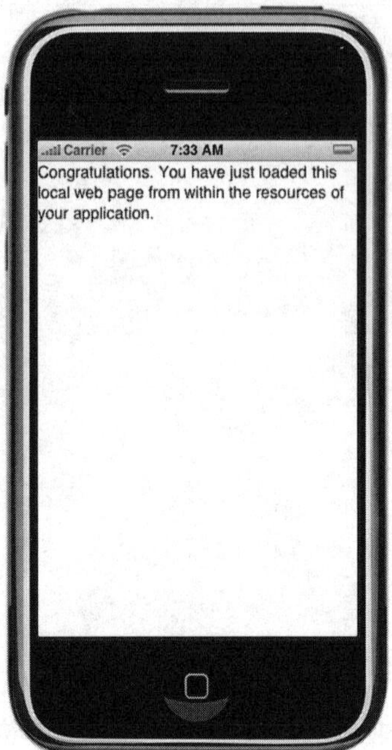

Figure 1.4 The default QuickConnect application

> **To Copy or Not to Copy Is the Question**
>
> Whether you copy the existing files or have Xcode use references to them is up to you. How do you decide? Each method has its advantages.
>
> If you copy the files, the project directory is complete and can be passed to other developers who do not need to replicate the directory structure of the machine that holds the existing files.
>
> If you use the reference method, you can go back into Dashcode to make changes, and then export the project to overwrite the files. You do not have to import them again into Xcode.

Next, right-click the Parts group and import the files in the Parts folder. Repeat this for the Images group and the Images folder, and you are almost ready to run the application.

Because files were added to the Resources group, Xcode needs to be told to include them in the resources used by the application. Expand the Targets selection near the bottom of the screen, and then expand your application and the Copy Bundle Resources listing. You can now see the resource files needed for your application to run. Select and drag the files (not the groups) that you just added to your project to this Copy Bundle Resources listing. Then, expand the Compile Sources list and remove any JavaScript files. They obviously won't be compiled. Do this by right-control clicking them, and then select Delete. This removes the files from the compilation list, but it does not delete the files from the project or disk.

Because Dashcode uses directories, and Xcode uses groups, you need to make two more changes to run your application. The first is in the `<head>` portion of the index.html file. Because the JavaScript files and any other files referenced exist in the resource directory of the final application, the directory references to `Parts` and `QCiPhone` must be removed. For example, before the reference is removed, a `<script>` tag will look like this:

```
<script type="text/javascript" src="Parts/utilities.js" charset="utf-8"></script>
```

Afterward, it should look like this:

```
<script type="text/javascript" src="utilities.js" charset="utf-8"></script>
```

Because images are used for any buttons, etc. that you created in Dashcode, you also need to locate instances of the string `Images/` in the entire project and replace them with empty strings. This is easily done by selecting the Edit pull-down menu, choosing Find → Find in Project, and then searching for `Images/`. Figure 1.5 shows the search results for this example prior to changing the PushButton.js file.

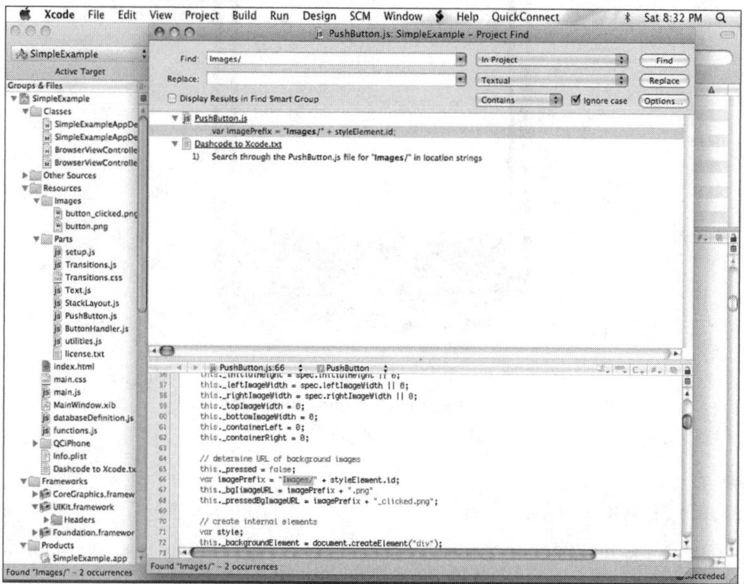

Figure 1.5 The search screen shows the results of the search for `Images/` in the entire project.

You can now install and run your application by selecting the Build and Go icon. It is in the top bar of the Xcode application. If you get the "No provisioned iPhone OS device is connected" error, you can install and run the application in the simulator instead of on your device. Click Succeeded in the bottom, right-hand corner of the Xcode window, select the *Device | Debug* pull-down list in the upper, left-hand corner of the dialog that displays, and click the *Simulator* selection. Notice that you can also choose Release or Debug further down the pull-down list. Use this dialog frequently during your development process to make these types of changes. Figure 1.6 shows the application installed and running in the simulator.

Congratulations. You just completed your first hybrid iPhone application.

Figure 1.6 The simpleExample application is installed and runs in the iPhone simulator.

> **Provisioning? What Is That?**
>
> Provisioning is the multistep process that you or someone representing you must do to enable you to install and run your application on a device.
>
> To provision your iPhone, you need to be a member of the Apple Developer Connection (ADC) and registered to use the Program Portal. If you are part of a team, the provisioning might be done already; if this is the case, you just need to upload the provisioning information to your iPhone.
>
> Copious information on how provisioning is done is available on the ADC. Be sure to follow all the steps listed. Any deviation can result in failure, preventing you from testing applications on your device.

Section 3: Using Xcode and the Custom PhoneGap Template

An Xcode custom PhoneGap application template is available and can be downloaded from https://sourceforge.net/projects/phonegapinstall. As with the QuickConnectiPhone installer, a custom template is available in the New → Project dialog; it is called PhoneGap Application. Double-click this icon, name your project, and save it to a location on your disk just as you did with the QuickConnectiPhone Application template.

> **Differences**
>
> One of the major differences between QuickConnectiPhone and PhoneGap is that PhoneGap applications do not include the HTML, CSS, and JavaScript files in the installed application. These files must reside on and be served up by a web server accessible via the Internet.
>
> If you choose to use PhoneGap, your application can be run only when the user has access to the Internet from his device. This is usually not a problem with iPhone owners, but it can be a major impediment to iPod Touch owners because they need to be near an open WiFi access point for Internet access.
>
> If you want your application installation to be complete, use QuickConnectiPhone. If you want the CSS, HTML, and JavaScript to reside remotely, you can use PhoneGap.

Because PhoneGap applications do not include the CSS, HTML, and JavaScript files in the installed application, you need to point it to a web server that contains these files. The simplest, temporary way to do this is on your own development machine.

Open your Sharing System Preference dialog and ensure that web sharing is activated. This turns your machine into a web server. In your <UserHome> → Sites directory, create a pg_hello directory and put an index.html file in it containing the following code:

```
<!DOCTYPE HTML PUBLIC "-//W3C//DTD HTML 4.01//EN"
      "http://www.w3.org/TR/html4/strict.dtd">
<html>
<head>
    <title>pg_example</title>
    <meta http-equiv="content-type" content="text/html; charset=utf-8">
    <meta name="viewport" content="minimum-scale=1.0, width=device-width, maximum-
scale=1.6">
</head>
<body>
Congratulations.  You have just loaded this web page from the Internet.
</body>
</html>
```

You must inform your PhoneGap application of the web server's location by modifying the url.txt file found in the Resources group. Because you have placed this file on your own machine, replace the text in the file with `http://localhost/~<user>/`

pg_hello where <user> is your login name. When you select the Build and Go icon in Xcode, your application compiles and displays the HTML page, as shown in Figure 1.7.

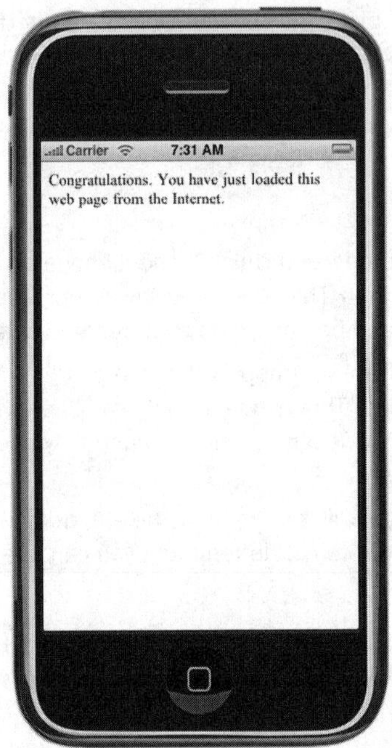

Figure 1.7 A running PhoneGap application

It is also possible to use Dashcode to create the HTML, CSS, and JavaScript for a PhoneGap application. This is done by starting Dashcode and double-clicking the Custom Web Application template. Add the same Text and Push Button elements, and create the listener for the button in the same way as the QuickConnectiPhone simpleExample application.

To make this an official PhoneGap application, you need to include the gap.js file found in the JavaScript directory of the PhoneGap download. Do this by right-control clicking the index.html file listing in Dashcode, and then selecting Add File.

Browse to the location of the unzipped PhoneGap download and select the gap.js file. In the <head> tag of the index.html file of your Dashcode project, add the following line of code:

```
<script type="text/javascript" src="gap.js" charset="utf-8"></script>
```

After you run and debug the code in Dashcode, you can deploy it to phoneGap-SimpleExample on your development machine's web server, run the PhoneGap Xcode application created earlier, and see the html page running in your embedded application (see Figure 1.8).

Figure 1.8
The PhoneGapSimpleExample application running

The same issues with provisioning and running on a development device apply to PhoneGap applications as they do QuickConnectiPhone applications. See Section 2 for more information on these topics.

Section 4: Introduction to Basic Objective-C

This section is not an in-depth Objective-C tutorial nor is it an in-depth discussion of how to use Objective-C to write iPhone applications. It does give an understanding of how the Objective-C classes used in the templates interact and behave, so that you can leverage this knowledge in iPhone hybrid applications. It also assumes that you have a basic understanding of objects, methods, and attributes. If you want to know more about the JavaScript framework or you don't want to know about Objective-C code, skip the rest of this chapter and go directly to Chapter 2. For a deeper understanding of Objective-C iPhone development, see *The iPhone Developer's Cookbook: Building Applications with the iPhone SDK* by Erica Sadun.

Objective-C is an interesting language. For readers with a background in JavaScript, PHP, Java, Perl, and other languages, it can seem daunting and incomprehensible at first glance. In spite of this, it does deserve a second glance and not just because it is the "native" language of the iPhone.

Objective-C is an object-oriented variant of C. You can do all the powerful, dangerous C/C++ type of programming you want, such as pointer arithmetic, and you can do some things to make your life easier, such as automated memory management. One of the first things you need to do in an object-oriented language is instantiate an object. If an object named **`Mammal`** is available in the source code named and has two attributes, *`furColor`* and *`milkFatRatio`*, in JavaScript, it is instantiated as shown in the following:

```
var aMammal = new Mammal("orange", 0.15);
```

You might think this is normal and expect other languages to behave in the same manner. Objective-C instantiation initially looks strange if you have that expectation. The same behavior in Objective-C looks like this:

```
Mammal *aMammal = [[Mammal alloc] initWithColor: @"orange" andMilkFatRatio: 0.15];
```

Some parts look comprehensible; others do not. If you think about it, the *`alloc`* makes sense because it is how the **`Mammal`** object is allocated space in RAM. Even the *`initWithColor`* and *`andMilkFatRatio`* make sense as setters or passers of the two needed parameters. However, what is actually going on and what do all those square brackets mean?

Objective-C uses message passing for all interactions with objects and other items that might not be objects in other languages as they are in Objective-C. Examine this line of code:

```
[Mammal alloc]
```

Earlier, it was hinted that this code fragment is where an object whose type is **`Mammal`** is allocated space in RAM. It is. The square brackets around **`Mammal`** and *`alloc`* indicate that the object in the application that represents the **`Mammal`** class is to be sent the *`alloc`* message. This code fragment is read as, *"Pass an `alloc` message to the **`Mammal`** class object."* The result of passing this *`alloc`* message to the **`Mammal`** class object is that a pointer to a new **`Mammal`** object is returned.

Pointers? What Are Those?

Pointers are interesting. Many people fear them because they don't understand them or don't know what they are.

To understand them, here is an analogy: Imagine a large crowd of people, and two people in the crowd are Alma and John. They know each other, and Alma knows where John is in the crowd. You approach Alma and ask her where John is. She points one finger at John and says, "There he is."

At this instant in time, Alma is a John pointer. If you think of a pointer as something that knows where an object is in memory, you understand.

This newly instantiated **Mammal** object can then be passed messages. The previous code snippet contains another message for this new **Mammal** object.

This new message consists of *initWithColor* and *andMilkFatRatio* combined together. You can tell that this two-part message is a message because it and the newly allocated **Mammal** are surrounded by square brackets, signifying that a message is being passed. Multipart messages are delimited by spaces. A space is between the two parts of the message.

In addition, the message parts and the values passed with them are linked together by the colon character (:). Each message part can have a maximum of one parameter associated with it. This passed message returns a pointer to the newly allocated **Mammal** object so it can be stored locally for later use. In Objective-C, these message indicators, whether for a single or multipart message, are called selectors because they indicate what methods of the object the compiler selects and runs.

Return to the *SimpleExample* Xcode project you created in Section 2. Look at the *applicationDidFinishLaunching* method in the *SimpleExampleAppDelegate.m* file that the template generated for you. Don't be concerned with what the code does. Look at it as an example of message passing.

```
1  - (void)applicationDidFinishLaunching:(UIApplication *)application {
2      // this helps in debugging, so that you know "exactly" where your views
are placed;
3      // if you see "red", you are looking at the bare window.
4      window.backgroundColor = [UIColor redColor];
5
6
7      QuickConnectViewController
8 *aBrowserViewController=[[QuickConnectViewController alloc] init];
9
10      // add the CreateViewController view to the window as subview
11      [window addSubview:aBrowserViewController.view];
12
13      [window makeKeyAndVisible];
14 }
```

Line 8 should look familiar. It doesn't involve mammals, but uses `alloc` and `init` messages you saw previously. In this case, something called a ***QuickConnectViewController*** is allocated and initialized. Its class object is passed the `alloc` message that returns a pointer to the newly allocated ***QuickConnectViewController***. This new object, via its pointer, is sent the `init` message.

This message accomplishes the same thing as the ***Mammal's*** multipart `initWithColor:andMilkFatRatio` message, but is much simpler. It is a single-part message and has no parameters. Later in this chapter, you see how to create initialization and other methods so that your objects can execute them when they are sent a message.

Line 11 sends a message to the `window`. This `addSubView` message has a parameter sent with it that is the `aBrowserViewController` object's contained `view` attribute.

You have now seen a usable example of how to instantiate an object, how to store a locally scoped pointer to this new object, how to access an object's attributes, and how to pass messages with and without parameters to objects. This is most of the basic Objective-C you need to know to understand the code in the QuickConnectiPhone and PhoneGap template files. Next, you need to understand how Objective-C applications are put together.

Section 5: Objective-C QuickConnectiPhone Application Structure

Although this section covers some of the basic code in the QuickConnectiPhone application template, the same approach is used in PhoneGap and all other hybrid application implementations. You can use either of these existing implementations or, by studying them, create your own version.

Imagine you have a large number of shares in a successful company, which might be true. Imagine there was a stockholder meeting to elect the chairman of the board, but you could not attend because you were on vacation in the Bahamas. How could you still cast your vote?

If you legally assign someone to vote for you, this person is referred to as your proxy. As your proxy they have full authority to act on your behalf at the meeting. Your proxy could be called your delegate. This delegate would refer to you as the principal because you are the actual stockholder. Figure 1.9 displays this relationship. Objective-C iPhone applications use principal-delegate relationships between objects where one is the principal and the other is the delegate.

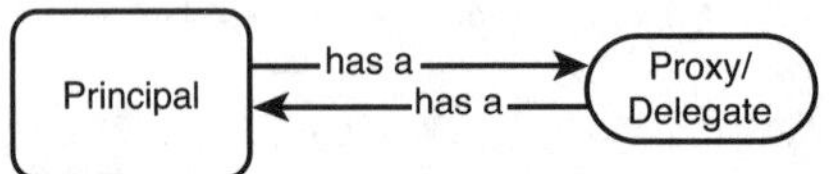

Figure 1.9 A graphical representation shows a principal has a delegate, and a delegate has a principal.

Objective-C iPhone applications use this principal-delegate relationship a lot. The principal-delegate relationships of interest are

- UIApplication/UIApplicationDelegate
- UIWebView/UIWebViewDelegate
- UIAccelerometer/UIAccelerometerDelegate

At this point, you need to understand that implementing protocol methods for these delegates tells your application, view, or accelerometer that you want the delegate to handle specific events when they occur instead of itself. Each protocol method is associated with one event.

Protocols

A protocol is a series of methods that can be added to a class, so that the class responds to specific messages.

With these principal-delegate concepts fresh in your mind, take a look at a class that is a delegate. Following is the header file for the `SimpleExampleAppDelegate` class that was generated when you used the QuickConnectiPhone Application template and created the SimpleExample application in Section 2.

Objective-C header files, the ones ending in .h, declare classes. Look at the header file for the `SimpleExampleAppDelegate` class, but don't worry about its implementation file:

```
1 //SimpleExampleAppDelegate.h
2 #import <UIKit/UIKit.h>
3 #import "QuickConnectViewController.h"
4
5 @interface  SimpleExampleAppDelegate : NSObject
6 <UIApplicationDelegate> {
7     IBOutlet UIWindow *window;
8     QuickConnectViewController *browserViewController;
9 }
10
11 @property (nonatomic, retain) UIWindow *window;
12 @property (nonatomic, retain) QuickConnectViewController
*browserViewController;
13
14 @end
```

Look at line 5. If you are familiar with Java, don't let the *`@interface`* indicator mislead you. It does not mean this class is like a Java interface. It means that this file contains the interface definition for this class. This header file declares what attributes `SimpleExampleAppDelegate` has, how they are accessible, and what methods are to be implemented in the separate implementation file. This class has no methods of its own.

If it is not a Java-like interface declaration, what then does line 5 do? It declares the name of the class as `SimpleExampleAppDelegate` and uses the colon delimiter to indicate that it inherits from the `NSObject` class. It is therefore an `NSObject` and can accept any ***`NSObject`***-defined messages. If you look at the `NSObject` class in the API documentation in the Xcode help menu, you can see that it has a `description` method; therefore, because `SimpleExampleAppDelegate` is an `NSObject` by inheritance, it also has a `description` method.

Next to the `NSObject` inheritance declaration, you can see *`<UIApplicationDelegate>`*. This is what tells the `SimpleExampleAppDelegate` class to behave as a delegate for your application and what enables you to implement the methods of the `UIApplicationDelegate` protocol messages in `SimpleExampleAppDelegate`'s implementation file. One method of this protocol is `applicationDidFinishLaunching`.

This method gets called just as the application completes loading and is ready to run. The method enables you to customize your application or query the user for more information if needed.

In the following code, line 11 has the QuickConnectiPhone's definition of `applicationDidFinishLaunching` in the implementation file. It starts with a minus (-) sign. This indicates it is an object method. The `(void)` means the method returns nothing, and `:(UIApplication *)application` indicates that one parameter of type `UIApplication` is passed into the method.

```
1 //
2 //  SimpleExampleAppDelegate.m
3 //  SimpleExample
4 //
5 #import "SimpleExampleAppDelegate.h"@implementation
6 SimpleExampleAppDelegate
7
8 @synthesize window;
9 @synthesize browserViewController;
10
11 - (void)applicationDidFinishLaunching:(UIApplication *)application {
12     // this helps in debugging, so that you know
13     // "exactly" where your views are placed;
14     // if you see "red", you are looking at the
15     // bare window, in your distributed applications
16     // use black
17   window.backgroundColor = [UIColor redColor];
18             QuickConnectViewController
19 *aBrowserViewController=[[QuickConnectViewController alloc] init];
20        // add the aBrowserViewController view to the
21    // window as a subview
22       [window addSubview:aBrowserViewController.view];
23    //[window makeKeyAndVisible];
24 }
```

This `applicationDidFinishLaunching` method, as part of the delegate class for your application, is called automatically when the application has completed loading. Because of this, it can be used to instantiate other items that might be needed in the application. In this case, you can see on lines 18 and 19 the allocation and initialization of the other class (`QuickConnectViewController`) included in your application by the template.

iPhone applications are view-based, and any `UIWindow` or `UIView` object can contain `UIView` objects. Therefore, it is possible to have a view within a view within a view. You are discouraged from using this type of design for iPhone applications. Instead of this heierarchical approach most of the developer community swaps one subview with another at as high a level as possible based on what the user needs.

Swapping subviews also flattens and reduces the complexity of your application's view structure. Thankfully, the template you used to create this application has placed just the right number of views within views for you to display your web content. In fact, as seen later, it inserted a web subview into the view that was just added to the window object.

The `QuickConnectViewController` class has the actual view object that displays your content in the window of your application as one of its attributes. This attribute needs to be added to the main window as a subview, which is done on line 22.

In addition to containing the content view, the `QuickConnectViewController` class is also a delegate. It is the delegate for the GPS location, accelerometer, WebView, and other types of events.

Section 6: Objective-C PhoneGap Application Structure

As iPhone applications, PhoneGap applications also follow the same principal-delegate structure as QuickConnectiPhone applications. See Section 5 for more information. The delegate class you need to understand is called `GlassAppDelegate`. Just like the `SimpleExampleAppDelegate` examined in Section 4, it has definition and implementation files. These are called GlassAppDelegate.h and GlassAppDelegate.m, respectively.

The `GlassAppDelegate` class in PhoneGap applications is much more than just an application delegate. It is the delegate for all types of behavior, so the .h and .m files are much more complex.

In the following code, you can see that the `GlassAppDelegate` class is a delegate for the WebView display, the GPS location manager, the accelerometers, and others. This is because these delegates are listed in a comma-delimited manner in the interface declaration starting on line 16.

```
1 #import <UIKit/UIKit.h>
2 #import <CoreLocation/CoreLocation.h>
3 #import <UIKit/UINavigationController.h>
4
5 #import "Vibrate.h"
6 #import "Location.h"
7 #import "Device.h"
8 #import "Sound.h"
9 #import "Contacts.h"
10
11
12 @class GlassViewController;
13 @class Sound;
14 @class Contacts;
15
16 @interface  GlassAppDelegate : NSObject <
17 UIApplicationDelegate,
```

```
UIWebViewDelegate,
CLLocationManagerDelegate,
UIAccelerometerDelegate,
UIImagePickerControllerDelegate,
UIPickerViewDelegate,
UINavigationControllerDelegate
>
{


    IBOutlet UIWindow *window;
    IBOutlet GlassViewController *viewController;
    IBOutlet UIWebView *webView;
    IBOutlet UIImageView *imageView;
    IBOutlet UIActivityIndicatorView *activityView;

    CLLocationManager *locationManager;
    CLLocation          *lastKnownLocation;

    UIImagePickerController *imagePickerController;

    NSURLConnection *callBackConnection;
    Sound *sound;
    Contacts *contacts;
    NSURL* appURL;
}

@property (nonatomic, retain) CLLocation *lastKnownLocation;
@property (nonatomic, retain) UIWindow *window;
@property (nonatomic, retain) GlassViewController *viewController;
@property (nonatomic, retain) UIImagePickerController
   *imagePickerController;

- (void) imagePickerController:(UIImagePickerController *)picker
   didFinishPickingImage:(UIImage *)image2 editingInfo:(NSDictionary
   *)editingInfo;
- (void) imagePickerControllerDidCancel:(UIImagePickerController
   *)picker;
@end
```

Although the `GlassAppDelegate` is more complex, the class is similar to the `SimpleExampleAppDelegate` class from the previous section. It is the delegate for the application and the delegate for other types of events, whereas theQuickConnectiPhone implementation uses the `QuickConnectViewController` class as the delegate for any events that are not except application delegate events.

The `SimpleExampleAppDelegate` method is the same as the one implemented in the `SimpleExampleAppDelegate`. In the interest of clarity, only some of the PhoneGap source code for the `applicationDidFinishLaunching` method is shown in the following. The source code left out is covered in detail in Section 9 and in Chapter 7, "Database Access."

```
1 -(void)applicationDidFinishLaunching:
    .
    .
    .
2     webView.delegate = self;
    .
    .
    .
3      [window addSubview:viewController.view];
    .
    .
    .
4 }
```

Line 2 of the code is interesting. Just as in the SimpleExampleAppDelegate implementation seen in Section 6, this sets a UIWebView to be a subview of the main window. This means that the UIWebView is used as the display for the entire application.

Having seen implementations of the main application delegate method in both QuickConnectiPhone and PhoneGap, you are ready to see how the UIWebView is used to display and run a JavaScript application.

Section 7: Embedding Web Content: QuickConnectiPhone

To display web content, such as JavaScript applications or simple web pages, in your application, you must use the `UIWebView` class. All implementations of hybrid applications, including QuickConnectiPhone and PhoneGap, use this class. If you want to do any fancy font control in an application—that is, multiple fonts and/or sizes and colors—you must use `UIWebView` unless you go through the painful process of drawing the text yourself. The `UIWebView` is much easier to use because it interprets HTML and CSS in addition to JavaScript. This enables you to easily do complex textual and other types of layouts.

The `UIWebView` class is actually a wrapper around the WebKit rendering engine that is used in the Safari browser, in Adobe Air, Android, and Nokia phones, and in several other applications including those shipped with OS X, such as Mail. Dashcode is also a heavy user of the WebKit engine.

As mentioned in the previous two sections, for a web view to be included in an application, the `UIWebView` object must be added as a subview to another view in the application. This is done in the `QuickConnectViewController` class's `loadView` method.

The `loadView` method contains a number of items that enable behaviors to be expressed in a JavaScript-based application. For example, the `loadView` method includes the code that scales your application's user interface to fit the size of the screen. This capability is commented out by default because the user interface should be designed to fit.

The interesting portion of `loadView` enables the display of the interface you created in Dashcode earlier in this chapter. The code snippet that follows is how the iPhone inserts this content into the application. It begins with the calculation of the size and point of origin for the display of the `UIWebView`. This is done by retrieving the size and location of the application's display frame.

The `CGRect` structure known as `webFrame` contains this information and is generated by sending the `applicationFrame` message to the main screen of the application. All `CGRect` structures consist of two items: a `CGPoint` called origin that represents a top-left point's x and y location and a `CGSize` that represents how large the rectangle is. This is represented by a height and width:

```
CGRect webFrame = [[UIScreen mainScreen] applicationFrame];
webFrame.origin.y -= 20.0;
```

The x, y, width, and height of a `CGRect` are floating-point numbers used to store pixel counts. The second line in the previous code shows how to change a current value of the vertical position stored in the `webFrame` variable. It shifts the origin up by 20 pixels. This has to be done to cover a blank space left in the view for a nonexistent toolbar at the top of the display window.

This toolbar can be seen in many standard applications, such as the Settings application you use to configure your Wi-Fi connections. It has been removed from the templates to maximize the use of the limited screen space available to the application. If you would like to have the next and previous behaviors of this bar, you should create it as part of your application using Dashcode.

When the `webFrame` has the location and size desired for the display of your web content, it is used to initialize a `UIWebView` object called `aWebView`. In the following code, Lines 1 and 2 show how this is done. Notice that it is similar to the `QuickConnectViewController` allocation examined earlier in this chapter. The major differences are that the `alloc` message is sent to the `UIWebView` class, and the `UIWebView` object that was just allocated is sent the `initWithFrame` message and passed the `webFrame` structure that was created and modified in the previous code snippet. The `aWebView` object is located and sized to the values contained in `webFrame`.

```
1 UIWebView *aWebView = [[UIWebView alloc]
2                 initWithFrame:webFrame];
3 self.webView = aWebView;
4 aWebView.autoresizesSubviews = YES;
5 aWebView.autoresizingMask=(UIViewAutoresizingFlexibleHeight
6                 | UIViewAutoresizingFlexibleWidth);
7 //set the web view delegate for the web view to be itself
8 [aWebView setDelegate:self];
```

This new `UIWebView` is stored in the `QuickConnectViewController`'s `webView` attribute by the code in line 4 so that it can be accessed later by other `QuickConnectViewController` methods. This becomes vital when using the acceleration, GPS location, and other capabilities described in Chapter 4, "GPS, Acceleration, and Other Native Functions with QuickConnect."

Lines 5 and 6 indicate what level of flexibility the `aWebView` object has to redraw itself. Avoid adding subviews if you can. Line 4 states that as `aWebView` changes size, so should the subviews. As the line is written, if `aWebView`'s width changes due to a rotation, any subview it contains should also change width by the same scaling factor.

Lines 5 and 6 indicate that the width and the height of `aWebView` will also change. When the iPhone is rotated, it is common for the current view to rotate to or from landscape mode and for the current view to resize itself to match the new width and height available from the device. If lines 5 and 6 are removed or commented out, the application still rotates but does not change the width and height of `aWebView`. This causes a large, blank area to appear to the right of the applications in landscape mode. Rarely should you allow your application's view to rotate without resizing itself.

Line 8 of the previous code sends `aWebView` a message stating that the current `QuickConnectViewController`, known as `self`, acts as the `aWebView` object's delegate. This enables the implementation of several optional `UIWebViewDelegate` methods in the `QuickConnectViewController` class. Table 1.1 indicates what these methods are.

Add each of these optional methods to the `QuickConnectViewController` class if you have a need. The template has already added `webView:shouldStartLoadWithRequest`, `webView:DidStartLoad`, `webView:DidFinishLoad`, and `webView:didFailLoadWithError`.

Having prepared `aWebView`, it is now appropriate to indicate what content it should load and then triggers the load. To accomplish this, the location of the index.html file located in the resources of the application must be determined. Thankfully, as seen in lines 3 and 4 of the code snippet, the `NSBundle` class that represents your application on disk has a method called `pathForResource:ofType`.

The `pathForResource:ofType` method takes two strings as parameters. The first is the name of the file shown as the string `index`, and the second is the file name extension `html`. The result of this call is that a full path to the file on your machine is generated and stored in the `filePathString` local variable. This string can then be used to create an object that represents a URL to the file and then the `NSURLRequest` object `aRequest` that represents the item you want to load, as seen on lines 7 and 8:

```
1 //determine the path the to the index.html file in the
2 //Resources directory
3 NSString *filePathString = [[NSBundle mainBundle]
4             pathForResource:@"index" ofType:@"html"];
5 //build the URL and the request for the index.html file
6 NSURL *aURL = [NSURL fileURLWithPath:filePathString];
7 NSURLRequest *aRequest = [NSURLRequest
8                              requestWithURL:aURL];
```

Table 1.1 **The UIWebView API**

Method Signature	When Called	Parameters
-(BOOL)webView:(UIWebView *) webView shouldStartLoadWithRequest: (NSURLRequest *) request navigationType: (UIWebViewNavigationType) navigationType	Just before the view starts loading content	webView—The view that is about to load content. request—The location of the content to be loaded. navigationType—The type of user action that causes the page to be loaded. UIWebViewNavigationType options—LinkClicked, FormSubmitted, BackForward, Reload, FormResubmitted, and Other.
- (void)webViewDidStartLoad: (UIWebView *) webView	After the view starts loading content	webView—The view that loads the content.
- (void)webViewDidFinishLoad: (UIWebView *) webView	After the view completes loading content successfully	webView—The view that loads the content.
- (void)webView:(UIWebView *) webView didFailLoadWithError:(NSError *) error	If the view fails to load the content	webView—The view that attempts to load the content. Error—An error object representing the error that occurred.

```
9     //load the index.html file into the web view.
10 [aWebView loadRequest:aRequest];
11     //add the web view to the content view
12 [contentView addSubview:aWebView];
```

In line 6, the `NSURL` object is passed the `fileURLWithPath` message. Because a file is loaded directly from disk, this is the appropriate message. This is is the only thing needed for QuickConnectiPhone hybrid applications, but if you use another implementation and load a page directly from the web, the message is `URLWithString`. It is passed with a full URL parameter such as http://www.byui.edu.

Having completed the creation of a `NSURLRequest` object, the actual loading of the requested URL is triggered by sending the `UIWebview` object `aWebView` the `loadRequest` message. The `NSURLRequest`, `aRequest`, is passed as the only parameter to this message.

After a request has been loaded, `aWebView` is added to the main content view by sending it the `addSubview` message with the UIWebView object passed as the parameter. If this is not done, the page is loaded and fully active, but it is not displayed.

Section 8: Embedding Web Content: PhoneGap

Unlike QuickConnectiPhone, PhoneGap sets up the location of the HTML file in the `applicationDidFinishLaunching` delegate method discussed in Section 6. Yet, much of what is done to display web content in your application is the same.

Just like the QuickConnectiPhone discussion in the previous section, PhoneGap must get a path to a file in the application distribution. This time the file is url.txt instead of QuickConnect's index.html. This is done in lines 8–12 of the following code.

First, as seen in the last section, the `NSBundle` object representing your application on disk is created. The `pathForResource` message is then passed to it with the parameter values `url` and `txt`. If this file is successfully located, `theURLString` local variable is assigned a string that is the content of the url.txt file, as seen on lines 14 and 15.

```
1 NSString * htmlFileName;
2 NSString * urlFileName;
3     htmlFileName = @"index";
4 urlFileName = @"url";
5     NSString * urlPathString;
6 NSBundle * thisBundle = [NSBundle bundleForClass:
7                          [self class]];
8     if (urlPathString = [thisBundle
9         pathForResource:urlFileName     ofType:@"txt"]) {
10     NSString * theURLString =
11                 [NSString stringWithContentsOfFile:
12                          urlPathString];
13     appURL = [NSURL URLWithString:theURLString];
14     [appURL retain];
15     NSURLRequest * aRequest =
16             [NSURLRequest requestWithURL:appURL];
17     [webView loadRequest:aRequest];
18 }
```

Line 13 converts the string retrieved from the url.txt file to a `NSURL` object that can be used to create a request. This request is, just as we saw in the previous section, passed as a parameter to `webView` using the `loadRequest` message.

With these two different implementations of the same behavior, you can see that although they are slightly different, they are mostly the same. All implementations of hybrid applications use the following approach:

1. Get a URL string.
2. Create an `NSURL` from the string.

3. Create an `NSURLRequest` from the `NSURL`.
4. Use the `UIWebViewloadRequest` message with the `NSURLRequest` as the parameter.

If you choose to write your own implementation, follow the same steps.

Summary

To create hybrid iPhone applications, you need a small Objective-C wrapper for your HTML, CSS, and JavaScript application. Dashcode is a powerful tool that enables you to quickly and easily create a dynamic JavaScript application that can be embedded using such a wrapper. Both the QuickConnectiPhone Application templates for Dashcode and Xcode and the PhoneGap template for Xcode speed up your application creation by including the repetitive code used in hybrid applications in your project. As Chapters 3, 4, 6, 7, and 8 show, the Xcode templates provide the Objective-C and JavaScript you need to write hybrid applications that include JavaScript access to the following:

PhoneGap

- Accelerometer data
- GPS location data
- Device vibration

QuickConnectiPhone

- Accelerometer data
- GPS location data
- Device vibration
- Custom system sounds
- Audio recording and playback
- Displaying standard Date and Date/Time pickers
- SQLite database access to databases shipped with your application and those in the UIWebView as the application runs

With the Dashcode and Xcode templates, you can create applications on the iPhone faster than ever before.

2

JavaScript Modularity and iPhone Applications

Usually, when writing JavaScript, two phrases come to mind: cross-browser compatibility and complexity. This chapter shows you how to avoid complexity in hybrid iPhone applications, and supplies you with source code that accomplishes complex behavior quickly and easily without sacrificing flexibility. With iPhone hybrid applications, you do not need to worry about cross-browser compatibility because only the Safari engine called WebKit is used. This makes it even easier to write interesting and fun JavaScript applications.

Section 1: Modularity

The concept of modularity has been around for a long time in both the computing and noncomputing industries. The essence of modularity is captured in the phrase, "Build it out of interchangeable pieces." If pieces are truly interchangeable modules, they must be capable of replacing each other with no, or almost no, changes to the items that interact with them. In software, this is usually a common, defined API that doesn't change.

The entertainment industry would be chaotic if each film was produced on a different medium because a different projector would be needed for each film. If an automobile manufacturer didn't standardize the way its engines were connected to the transmissions, each engine-transmission combination would have to be hand crafted. Costs would skyrocket and quality could easily crash. In the software industry, many attempts have been made to create modular, reusable code. Today, these are referred to as frameworks.

> **Module Defined**
>
> For a module to exist, it must have two characteristics: tight cohesion and loose coupling.
>
> Tight cohesion means the modular item has a clearly defined role and that it does everything needed to fulfill this role. It has a purpose for its existence and it acts on that purpose, such as handling one activity.

> Loose coupling means the module isn't reliant on knowing the internal workings of other modules, and no other modules know about its internal workings either. This requires the creation and use of a strong interface.
>
> When these two characteristics are achieved, a module is born.
>
> A steak is a module; spaghetti is not.

Frameworks are interesting to examine. There is usually a tradeoff between a framework's ease of use and its flexibility. If the framework developer isn't careful, he can make doing unimportant things with the framework easy and doing what the engineer or programmer needs to do hard.

Often, in the attempt to make a framework easy to use and flexible, execution scalability is sacrificed, which is the issue with Ruby on Rails. It is great to use but won't scale to enterprise sizes without large amounts of clustered hardware, which reduces its supportability and increases its cost. So, how can a framework be scalable, easy to use, and flexible? The answer is well-applied and highly engineered modularity.

Although not usually taught or emphasized, certain types of modules help make software development easier. These somewhat secret modules are known as front controllers and application controllers.

The examples in this chapter show you how to create and use these modules and how they can make your application creation easier and faster.

Section 2: The QuickConnect JavaScript Framework—A Modularity Example

The JavaScript framework in the Dashcode and Xcode templates is designed to minimize CPU and RAM usage and still be easy to use. Because this framework is designed to be highly modular, each component does one thing, does it well, and does it quickly.

The design uses a command-response paradigm. When you send a command, the modules run the necessary functions associated with the command. Figure 2.1 shows how this processing flows through an application using this design approach. Processing begins at step 1 and follows the numbered arrows through the framework.

The only items in the flow that are not already created are the Validation, Business, and View Control Functions specific to your application's behavior. Examples of these application specific modules are given throughout the remainder of this book.

To validate user input, use Validation Control Functions (ValCF). Use Business Control Functions (BCF) to retrieve data from a database, a web server, or another source, or to put it into storage. Use View Control Functions (VCF) to update the user viewable screen.

For example, you might want to gather user information with a form-like interface that includes a Submit button. Then, you can store this information in the SQLite database and indicate to the user that the data was stored successfully.

To do this, create three control functions: a Validation Control Function to ensure that the entered data meets the minimum standards required by your application, a Business

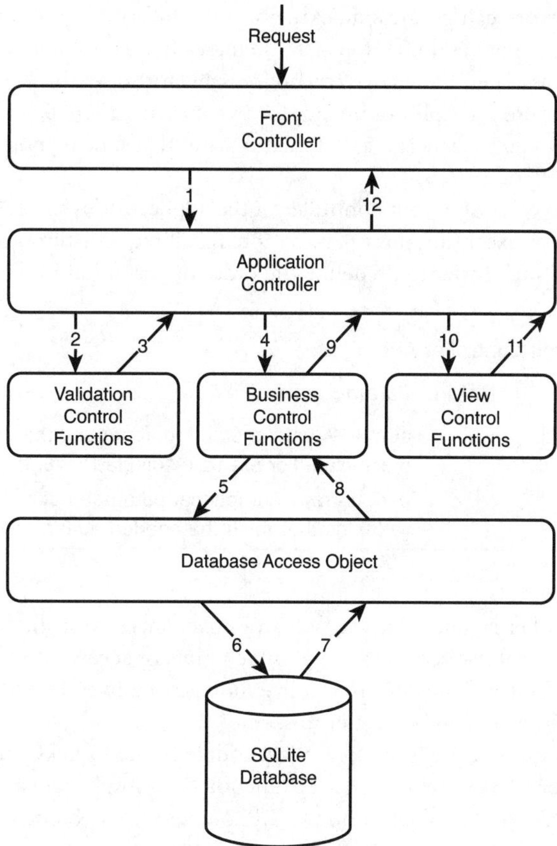

Figure 2.1 The processing flow associated with a single command

Control Function to store the information in the database, and a VCF to trigger a viewable success message.

Not all functionality needs to be associated with all three types of control functions. An application such as a game usually does not need to have a ValCF each time the user triggers some sort of behavior.

Figure 2.1 indicates that you do not need to make each of these different control functions communicate with each other. The framework modules are designed to do that work. You just need to write your control functions and associate them with commands. Because of the design, each of the control functions requires few lines of code and is immediately functional.

Because the design is modular, you can easily apply the concept of division of labor. If you divide the creation of these control functions in a team either by command or by type, independent work can progress quickly. For more information about what each of these control functions are and how to create them, see Sections 4 and 5.

Control functions, when done correctly, are reusable for more than one command. For example, you might use multiple commands for updating the same portion of the screen. This design enables you to associate a VCF that updates that specific portion of the view with any number of commands.

As shown in Table 2.1, the front controller of the application is the gateway through which all requests for execution must pass. By forcing all requests through the front controller, it becomes much easier to predefine the order of execution in the application.

Table 2.1 **The FrontController API**

Method Signature	Return	Parameters
handleResult(aCmd, paramArray)	void	aCmd—A unique string representing the behavior you want processed. For example "displayBlogEntries." paramArray—An optional parameter consisting of an array of variables that might be needed during processing.

The front controller is much like the wall around an ancient fortified town: only one way in and one way out. By reducing the possible points of access into the town, it becomes easier to defend and the citizens can live more secure lives. Including a front controller in your application makes it easier to secure.

The implementation of the front controller module in the QuickConnectiPhone JavaScript framework is the `handleRequest` function. This implementation is found in the QuickConnect.js file in your application's QCiPhone group in Xcode or QCiPhone folder in Dashcode. By examining the code, you can see how it performs its security and execution order functions.

When the `handleRequest` function is called, it is passed a command and an array of parameters. The command parameter is required but the paramArray is optional.

The following code, located in lines 17–20 in the functions.js file of the simpleCalc application, is an example of calling the `handleRequest` function in response to a user action. Here, the user clicks the addition symbol button. Figure 2.2 shows the simpleCalc application after the user presses the Multiply button.

```
function add(event)
{
    handleRequest('math',new Array('+'));
=}
```

The `math` command is passed as the first parameter, and an array containing the single character + is passed as the second parameter. Using an array as the second parameter might seem unnecessary in this instance, but because the design requires an array as the second parameter, it is more flexible as you see later in this chapter.

Figure 2.2 The simpleCalc example application shows the result of pressing the Multiply button.

The `add` function is the `onclick` listener for a button. When the associated button is selected, all ValCFs, BCFs, and VCFs mapped to the `math` command are executed and the parameter array is passed to them. Notice that the `subtract`, `multiply`, and `divide` listener functions also use the same command as `add`, but pass a different character in the array.

In this case, the application reuses the same ValCF, BCF, and VCF code for each piece of functionality. It is possible to use a different command in each listener and different BCFs, and then reuse the ValCFs and VCFs. In that case distinct BCFs for each type of arithmetic operation desired would be needed but they would be similar. Thus, a design decision was made to create only one BCF in this case.

Figure 2.3 shows the application flow in the simpleCalc example when a user selects any of the arithmetic buttons in the user interface. In this example, two ValCFs are executed to determine if it is safe to continue processing. Remember that the modular design shown here enforces the order of the function calls.

The first ValCF checks to ensure that the two values entered by the user are numbers. The second, `divisionByZeroValCF`, ensures that division by zero cannot happen.

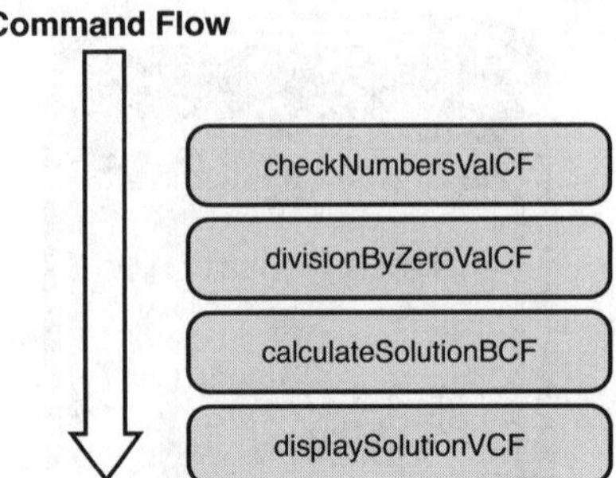

Figure 2.3 Execution order of the control functions mapped to the `math` command

After passing both validations, the `calculateSolutionsBCF` function is called. This BCF performs the arithmetic calculation requested by the user. The `displaySolutionVCF` then shows the result (refer to Figure 2.2).

If, however, the request fails to pass either ValCF, the modular design presented has control functions to handle this situation.

Error Control Functions (ECF) are defined as control functions used to handle error situations. If either ValCF fails, the `entryECF` function is called (see Figure 2.4). This function notifies the user about an error with one or more of the entries.

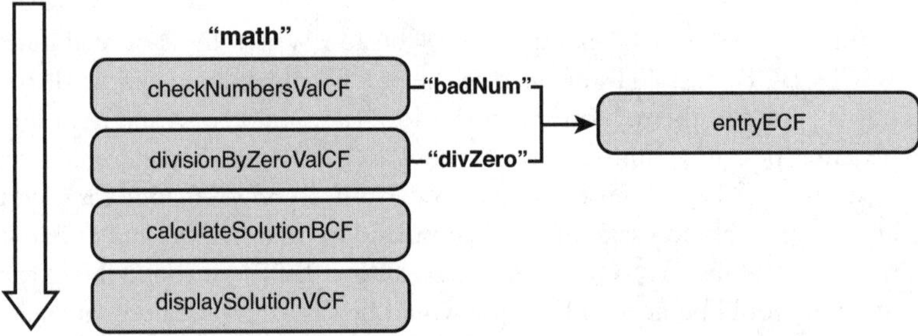

Figure 2.4 The command flow design of the `math` command

How, then, is the `math` command mapped to the four command functions that need to be executed? Four utility functions are provided in the QuickConnectiPhone implementation of this design. Each of them, as shown in Table 2.2, maps a command to a control function.

Table 2.2 **The Mapping Function API**

Method Signature	Return	Parameters
MapCommandToValCF(command, validationControlFunction)	Void	command—A unique string representing the behavior you want processed. For example `math`. validationControlFunction—A validation function to execute when the command is received by the `handleRequest` function.
MapCommandToBCF(command, businessControlFunction)	Void	command—A unique string representing the behavior you want processed. For example `math`. businessControlFunction—A business function to execute when the command is received by the `handleRequest` function.
MapCommandToVCF(command, viewControlFunction)	Void	command—A unique string representing the behavior you want processed. For example `math`. viewControlFunction—A view function to execute when the command is received by the `handleRequest` function.
MapCommandToECF(command, errorControlFunction)	Void	command—A unique string representing the behavior you want processed. For example `divZero`. errorControlFunction—An error function to execute when the command is received by the `handleRequest` function.

The following code, found in lines 24–27 of the mappings.js file, shows how mapping commands to control functions is done for the `math` command and the two error commands `badNum` and `divZero`.

```
//mapping one command to multiple funcitons
 mapCommandToValCF('math',checkNumbersValCF);
 mapCommandToValCF('math',divisionByZeroValCF);
 mapCommandToBCF('math', calculateSolutionBCF);
 mapCommandToVCF('math', displaySolutionVCF);

 //multiple commands mapped to one function
 mapCommandToECF('badNum', entryECF);
 mapCommandToECF('divZero', entryECF);
```

A well-designed front controller needs to be only written once and can be reused in multiple applications. The specific front controller-application controller design presented in this chapter also provides a simple way to design the specific behaviors of your applications.

Because this full design ensures that all validation control functions execute first followed by all BCFs and VCFs, it becomes easy to layout the function-level design of your application (see Figure 2.4).

This full framework design also ensures that the control functions execute in the order that they are mapped to commands. In the previous mapping code, the `checkNumbersValCF` function is always called before the `divisionByZeroValCF`.

Application Controllers

An application controller, based on the standard application controller pattern, exists to map commands to a specific functionality. As such, implementations of the pattern generally consist of a map that has commands as the keys and functionality targets as the values.

In this chapter's design, the values associated with the map's keys are lists of functions. This enables the controller to execute multiple functions in the specified order and increase the modularity and reusability of the control function targets.

A well-designed application controller makes your application extensible because functionality can be added without rewriting the interfunctional communication of your application. The QuickConnectiPhone application controller implementation is an example of this.

Now that you have seen how the commands are mapped to control functions, it is time to examine the creation of control functions. The `checkNumbersValCF` function is fairly typical of ValCFs. It is single task-oriented and ensures only that the values entered by the user are numeric. If they are not numeric, it calls one of the application controllers, `dispatchToECF`, to handle the error:

```
function checkNumbersValCF(parameters){
    //make sure both a and b are numbers
    var a = document.getElementById('a').value;
    var b = document.getElementById('b').value;
    if(isNaN(a) || isNaN(b)){
        dispatchToECF('badNum','Enter numbers only.');
        return false;
    }
    return true;
}
```

ValCFs return true if the situation correctly validates and false if it does not. This enables processing to stop immediately on failure, which increases the security of your application.

Earlier in this section, the `calculateSolutionBCF` mapped BCF to the `math` command. As with most BCFs, it retrieves data on which to act. In this case, it pulls the data from the user interface. In other cases, a BCF might pull values from a database or, using AJAX, pull it from a server on the Internet. This code shows the implementation of this BCF:

```
function calculateSolutionBCF(parameters){


    var a = document.getElementById('a').value;
    var b = document.getElementById('b').value;
```

```
    if(a == ''){
        a = 0;
    }
    if(b == ''){
        b = 0;
    }
    //evaluate the result of the calculation
    var expression = a+parameters[0]+b;
    var result = eval(expression);
    return new Array(a, b, result);

}
```

BCFs return an array of information rather than the boolean of ValCFs. This array can contain any information you choose to include. In this case, the two values that the user entered and the calculated result are returned because each of these needs to be used later to generate the information displayed to the user, as seen in Figure 2.2.

The actual calculation of the result uses JavaScript's `eval` function. This function attempts to execute any string as if it contains valid JavaScript code. In this example, if the user enters 3 and 5 for the values and selects the Multiply button, the `expression` variable contains the string "3*5." When this string is passed to `eval`, the result returned is 15.

Be careful when using the `eval` function because it executes any string it is given. In the simpleCalc example application, it is safe to use because the ValCF that ensures that both the `a` and `b` values are numbers has been passed. If validation hasn't been done on the elements used in a call to `eval`, users can discover the internals of an application and perform nefarious acts, such as an SQL insertion attack if the BCF has database access.

The `displaySolutionVCF` is a simple example of VCFs. As with the other control functions, it does one thing: It updates the display div with a string showing the arithmetic action performed and the calculated result:

```
function displaySolutionVCF(data, parameters){
    var result = data[0][0]+' '+parameters[0]
            +' '+data[0][1]+' = '+data[0][2];
    document.getElementById('display').innerHTML = result;
}
```

Generally, VCFs update the HTML of the main page in some way. An example of a major change of the view is changing out the entire viewable UI. This example makes a small change. It displays the arithmetic performed and leaves the rest of the UI unchanged.

ECFs can also be either simple or complex. They might involve behavior such as making changes to stored data or be as simple as the following `entryECF` example. It receives a string as its only parameter and displays it to the user:

```
function entryECF(message){
    document.getElementById('display').innerHTML = message;
}
```

Because of its simplicity, this ECF can be used in the case of validation failures in both ValCFs in this example application.

By using a good implementation of the front controller-application controller design, you can focus the application design and implementation on actual desired behavior rather than on interfunction communication/data passing. The next section shows an implementation of a front controller and application controllers.

Section 3: The QuickConnectiPhone Implementation of the Modular Design

The `handleRequest` function, like most other portions of the design implementation in this section, is small. It and the method for which it is a façade consist of 21 lines of code of which only 15 are active. In the following code, the lines of interest, 7–21, are bold.

Because `handleRequest` is the implementation of the front controller portion of the design discussed in the previous section, it is responsible for calling four application controllers. Each application controller is responsible for handling one type of the control functions. `dispatchToValCF` as shown in line 7 of the following code is the first application controller called. (Table 2.3 describes each application controller function.)

Table 2.3 **The Application Controller API**

Method Signature	Return	Parameters
dispatchToValCF (aCmd, paramArray)	Boolean. True on success; false on failure.	aCmd—A unique string representing the behavior you want processed. For example, `displayBlogEntries`. paramArray—An optional parameter consisting of an array of variables that are needed during processing.
dispatchToBCF(aCmd, paramArray, callBackData)	Data ready to be displayed or `stop`. If `stop` is returned, no further computation is done for the indicated command.	aCmd—A unique string representing the behavior you want processed. For example, `displayBlogEntries`. paramArray—An optional parameter consisting of an array of variables that are needed during processing. callBackData—An optional parameter generated by the framework if asynchronous calls are made from within any BCFs associated with the command.

Table 2.3 **The Application Controller API**

Method Signature	Return	Parameters
dispatchToVCF(aCmd, data, paramArray,)	Void	aCmd—A unique string representing the behavior you want processed. For example, `displayBlogEntries`. data—An array consisting of all of the data generated by calls to BCFs. paramArray—An optional parameter consisting of an array of variables that are needed during processing.
dispatchToECF(aCmd, errorMessage)	Void	aCmd—A unique string representing the behavior you want processed. For example, `databaseDown`. errorMessage—A message to notify the developer through logging or the user through display. This message should be descriptive and helpful to the type of target user it is intended for.

`dispatchToValCF` calls all of the ValCFs you have mapped to the command value in the `aCmd` variable. If the mapped validation functions pass, it returns a boolean value of true; if any one of the ValCFs fail, it returns false.

Because this `dispatchToValCF` call is wrapped in an if statement, further processing of your request happens only if it returns true. If it returns false, your request falls into the error-handling routine only if you have mapped ECFs to the main command. The simpleCalc example application, as shown earlier, has no such mapping.

```
function handleRequest(aCmd, paramArray){
    requestHandler(aCmd, paramArray, null);
}

function requestHandler(aCmd, paramArray, callBackData){
    if(aCmd != null){
        if(dispatchToValCF(aCmd, paramArray)){
        try{
            var data = dispatchToBCF(aCmd,
                paramArray, callBackData);
             if(data != 'stop'){
```

```
                    dispatchToVCF(aCmd, data, paramArray);
                }
            }
            catch(err){
                logError(err);
            }
            }
            else{
                dispatchToECF(aCmd, 'validation failed');
            }
    }
}
```

After your request passes validation, the front controller module calls the next application controller, `dispatchToBCF`. This controller function calls the BCFs you associated with the command to retrieve or store any data you desire.

If your BCF returns anything other than `stop`, the front controller calls the VCFs you also associated with the command. It accomplishes this by calling the third application controller, `dispatchToVCF`. For further information on BCFs and VCFs, see Section 4.

The purpose of the front controller module mentioned previously is to offer a quick and easy way to ensure a stable, secure, computational flow through your application. When a flow is consistently used, it is much easier to create and debug your applications. Therefore, when you use the QuickConnectiPhone implementation of the design, make calls to the `handleRequest` function when you want something to happen in your application.

Each application control function in Table 2.3 performs a distinct role and enables the handling of your command to continue or stop depending on the decisions you make in your ValCFs and BCFs. They are modules because they are reusable, loosely coupled, and tightly cohesive.

The `dispatchToValCF` function is a façade. This function and the `dispatchToSCF` function are the same behaviorally, but they work against different sets of data. Use ValCFs to validate input from the user. Security Control Functions (SCFs) are used to ensure that data retrieved from remote sources such as web sites doesn't contain nefarious code. Because of this similarity of function, it is best to centralize the working code and use façade functions to make the call to the underlying `check` function.

The following code, found in the QuickConnect.js file, shows the `dispatchToValCF` façade function and the underlying `check` function. As you can see, the `dispatchToValCF` function calls `check` and passes it its own two parameters plus an additional one. This additional parameter is a string describing the type of map the `check` function is to use. This map, or associative array, contains all of the associations between commands and an array of ValCFs. To create and associate commands with ValCFs, see Section 2 of this chapter.

```
function dispatchToValCF(validationCommand, paramArray){
    return check(validationCommand, 'validation', paramArray);
}

```

```
5 /*
6  * This function is not intended to be called directly by the programmer.  Do not use it.
7  */
8 function check(command, type, data){
9       var retVal = true;
10       /*
11        * execute all of the default functions that apply to all commands if there are any default functions defined.
12        */
13       var map = securityMap;
14       if(type == 'validation'){
15             map = validationMap;
16       }
17       var defaultFuncs = map['default'];
18       if(defaultFuncs){
19             var numFuncs = defaultFuncs.length;
20             for(var i = 0; i < numFuncs; i++){
21             retVal = defaultFuncs[i](command, data);
22                   if(retVal == false){
23                         break;
24                   }
25             }
26       }
27       /*
28        * if the default functions have passed, then do those specifically for the command
29        */
30      if(retVal == true){
31             commandFuncs = map[command];
32
33             if(commandFuncs){
34                   var numFuncs = commandFuncs.length;
35                   for(var i = 0; i < numFuncs; i++){
36                         retVal = commandFuncs[i](data);
37                         if(retVal == false){
38                               break;
39                         }
40                   }
41             }
42       }
43       return retVal;
44 }
```

In line 17, the code attempts to retrieve an array of control functions associated with the `default` command. The retrieval of these control functions means that you can create a VCF, and if you map it to `default`, it gets called for every command you send to `handleRequest`.

A common default ValCF is one that ensures that a mapping for the command being passed in exists in either the map for the BCFs, the VCFs, or both. If the command does not exist in these functions, there is no reason to continue processing the command, so it stops all further validation checking and returns `false`.

By returning `false`, it causes the `dispatchToValCF` function to immediately return `false`, too. This, in turn, causes the front controller to stop further processing. This ValCF catches unmapped, erroneous commands before they can cause problems later in your application.

If there are no default ValCFs or the command passes all those associated with the `default` command, the `check` method continues by retrieving the list of ValCFs associated with the specific command passed in and executes each one of them in order.

This prechecking of inputs of all types, as discussed in Section 2, is one of the purposes of the `dispatchToValCF` function and the ValCFs that you create. The prechecking also enables you to separate your validation code from your execution code. By creating this separation, you clarify both the validation code and execution code, making the ability to support your application simpler. It also aids you during the creation of the software by simplifying the design process (see Section 2).

Section 4: Business and View Application Controller Implementations

Of these two application controllers, business is the more complex and view is simple. The `dispatchToBCF` function calls all the BCFs mapped to a command even if one or more of the BCFs make asynchrounous calls. The `dispatchToVCF` function is much simpler because it looks much like the `displatchToValCF` function, and VCFs are never asynchronous. Even though both of these functions have a similar behavior, their implementations are dramatically different.

As discussed in Section 2, the `dispatchToBCF` business application control function is called only if the ValCFs you have defined and mapped indicate that it is safe to continue processing. Although this function uses some of the same ideas, it is significantly different than the `checkValidation` method.

The `dispatchToBCF` function consists of two major portions. The first portion contains lines 18–40 and deals with the `callBackData` array. This array represents the data that has been accumulated when an asynchronous call is made. If your BCF makes no asynchronous calls, this array is null. If it does make a call, such as an AJAX call or a call to retrieve data from a database, this array contains the data required to continue calling the remaining BCFs mapped to the command. Lines 25 and 31 show that this `callBackData` array includes the `results` of all BCFs called prior to the asynchronous call and the data generated by the asynchronous call itself.

> **Asynchronous Defined**
>
> In computing, you are used to thinking synchronously. To be synchronous means to do things one at a time in a defined order. When calling a function, the normal expectation is that each step of the function executes in order. When all steps are complete, the function returns some value or void.
>
> Asynchronous behavior is different from this. It is more like a soccer game. In a soccer game, each player is busy doing what needs to be done regardless of whether anyone else is also busy. It would be silly any other way. Imagine a game in which all players waited for other players to finish what they were doing before they started moving. Silly.
>
> Asynchronous computing behavior means that you can tell a function to do something, but processing continues without waiting to get anything back from the function.

Line 34 adds the data generated by the asynchronous call to the `results` array in those cases where no previous BCF call has been made. Thus, after this line executes, the `results` array appears to the rest of the code as if no asynchronous calls were made.

Line 37 retrieves the index number of the BCF that made the asynchronous call; otherwise, the remainder of the `dispatchToBCF` function would not know how many BCFs mapped to the command have already been executed. Asynchronous calls make a "break" in the execution of the BCFs mapped to the command. The `dispatchToBCF` function does not know which BCFs have already been executed unless an indicator is included in the data received from the results of the asynchronous call.

In Chapter 7, "Database Access," this is done for you by the getData, setData, getNativeData, and setNativeData methods of the `DataAccessObject`. If you create your own framework that enables asynchronous calls, create a set of code similar to the following:

```
1 function dispatchToBCF(aCmd, paramArray, callBackData){
2
3     if(event == null){
4         event = window.event;
5     }
6     if(event != null){
7         stopDefault(event);
8     }
9     window.curCmd = aCmd;
10     if(paramArray){
11         window.globalParamArray = paramArray;
12     }
13     else{
14         window.globalParamArray = new Array();
15     }
16       var results = new Array();
17     window.numFuncsCalled = 0;
18     if(callBackData){
19         if(callBackData[0]){
20             if(callBackData[1]){
```

```
            var accumulatedDataFromCallback =
                                callBackData[1][3];
            if(accumulatedDataFromCallback &&
                  accumulatedDataFromCallback.length > 0){
                results = accumulatedDataFromCallback;
            }
        }
        if(results.length == 0){
            //results should always be an array.
                     //The [] make sure that it is.
            results = [callBackData[0]];
        }
        else{
            results.push(callBackData[0]);
        }
    }
    if(callBackData[1]){
        window.numFuncsCalled = callBackData[1][1];
    }
}
var stop = false;
  if(aCmd){
        var commandList = businessMap[aCmd];
        callFunc = function(data){
              if(data){
                    results.append(data);
           window.globalBCFResults = results;
              }
              if(window.numFuncsCalled < commandList.length){
                    var funcToCall =
                          commandList[window.numFuncsCalled];
                    window.numFuncsCalled++;
                    var result = null;
                    try{
                          result = funcToCall(paramArray,
                                      results);
                    }
                    catch(err){
                          dispatchToECF('runFailure',
                                            err.message);
                    }

                    if(result != null){
                          results[results.length] = result;
                          callFunc();
                    }
            else{
```

```
68                     stop = true;
69                 }
70                   }
71             }
72             if(commandList && commandList.length > 0){
73                   callFunc();
74             }
75        }
76     if(stop){
77         return 'stop';
78     }
79     return results;
80 }
```

Lines 41–80 in the `dispatchToBCF` application control function illustrate how to do three things:

- Create and use anonymous JavaScript functions
- Do recursion in JavaScript
- Call the BCFs associated with a command

An anonymous function is any function that is created "on the fly" inside another function. The example used in the previous code is the `callFunc` function found on lines 44—71. This function does not exist outside of the `dispatchToBCF` function. As with all anonymous functions, it is strictly limited by the scope of the function within which it is declared. On the other hand, any variables declared within the containing function prior to the declaration of the anonymous function are still within scope and can be used in the anonymous function even though they are not passed as parameters.

Lines 43 and 44 are an example of this. The `commandList` variable is defined outside of the `callFunc` function, is not passed to the `callFunc`, and yet, it is used within the function. It is used on lines 50 and 51 to retrieve the next BCF to execute. Lines 55 and 56 execute this BCF and store the results of the call.

As an example of recursion, `callFunc` calls itself on line 65. This happens at the end of the function only if the result of the call to the BCF did not return null. This type of recursion is called tail recursion because the check is at the end of the function. If the check had been at the beginning of the function, it would be an example of head recursion. The full recursive cascade triggered by `callFunc` is started by the call on line 73.

Recursion

Recursion is the calling of a function by itself.

When the `dispatchToVCF` function is called a list of control functions is retrieved that are mapped to the command as seen in the code below. Unlike the validation application control function, `dispatchToVCF` is passed a data parameter that is an array consisting of elements that are the individual results of the calls to each of the BCFs.

Like the `dispatchToBCF` function, if any of the VCFs return stop, no further VCFs are executed. This enables programmers to terminate further execution if they make a call to `dispatchToECF`.

```
function dispatchToVCF(aCmd, data, paramArray){
    if(aCmd){
            var vcfFuncList = viewMap[aCmd];
            if(vcfFuncList == null){
                  vcfFuncList = new Array();
            }
        var numFuncs = vcfFuncList.length;
        for(var i = 0; i < numFuncs; i++){
                  try{
                        retVal = vcfFuncList[i](data, paramArray);
                  }
                  catch(err){
                        debug(errorMessage(err));
                  }
            if(retVal && retVal == 'stop'){
                break;
            }
        }
    }
}
```

When each VCF is retrieved, it is called and passed the BCF result data and the original parameters, `paramArray`, sent by your application to the `handleRequest` function. This is included in the implementation to enable you to pass information into both BCFs and VCFs called by the business and view application controllers.

Section 5: Error Application Controller Implementation

Unlike the other application controllers covered in Sections 3 and 4, the implementation of the error application controller found in the QuickConnectiPhone framework enables only one ECF to be mapped to a command. This means that each ECF must fully handle the error, which includes changing stored data, updating the view to notify the user, and so on.

The following implementation is an example of a simple error application controller:

```
function dispatchToECF(errorCommand, errorMessage){
    var errorFunc = errorMap[errorCommand];
    if(errorFunc){
        return errorFunc(errorMessage);
    }
}
```

This implementation simply retrieves the ECF to execute and passes the error message to the ECF. To activate error handling in this way, a call to `dispatchToECF` must be made directly, not via a call to `handleRequest`. The following line of code is found in the `checkNumbersValCF` function:

```
dispatchToECF('badNum','Enter numbers only.');
```

This call to `dispatchToECF` passes a message to be inserted into the display of the user interface informing the user that only numbers are acceptable values for entry.

Section 6: Application Functionality Creation Steps

Sections 3–5 explain what is happening behind the scenes when you use the QuickConnectiPhone framework's implementation of the front and application controller design. What are the steps that you need to execute in order to write most pieces of application functionality? They are as follows:

1. Create any BCFs to retrieve or store data, as shown in Section 4.
2. Create any VCFs to modify the user interface, as shown in Section 4.
3. Create any ValCFs needed for user input, as shown in Section 3.
4. Create any ECFs needed to handle possible error conditions, as shown in Section 5.
5. Map all of your new CFs to a command using the matching `mapCommandTo***` functions.

After you complete these five steps, the new functionality is part of your application.

Summary

Modularity makes your code easier to write, easier to maintain, and smaller in size when done appropriately. By keeping this and the speed of execution targets in mind, the QuickConnectiPhone framework's implementation provided to you in every application you create using the QuickConnectiPhone Application templates makes your life much easier. You get to focus on what you want to do which is to create and provide functionality for your users. The framework handles the interfunction communication and control for you.

By creating ValCFs, BCFs, VCFs, and ECFs, you can easily scope your work to increase productivity; at the same time, you increase the quality and security of your code.

3

Creating iPhone User Interfaces

The iPhone presents an opportunity for unique user-interaction methods. Older interface design methods are insufficient in this new medium. Your application can supply the user the intuitive interface interactions and interface elements that iPhone users demand. This chapter discusses how this can be done. It also discusses the Human Interface Guide from Apple that is used to evaluate applications for inclusion in the App Store. A drag-and-drop rotate scale module is also shown and explained to help you see how to handle touch and gesture events in JavaScript. These new types of JavaScript events are vital to iPhone user interface design.

Section 1: Apple's Human Interface Guide

To give iPhone users a common experience, Apple created a guide to what should be used in iPhone application user interfaces. This section gives you the flavor and highlights of the iPhone Human Interface Guide (HIG) in a short and straightforward manner. The full iPhone HIG is found at http://developer.apple.com/iphone/library/documentation/UserExperience/Conceptual/MobileHIG/Introduction/chapter_1_1.html.

The iPhone HIG is descended from interface guides created earlier for OS X and iPhone web development. There is a lot in common among these guides and iPhone's HIG. The new guide builds on the strengths of those that came before it and adds new iPhone application-specific coverage.

On the iPhone screen, space is so limited that textual output to the user can easily become overwhelming. For applications whose main function is not to read textual data, images and icons should be used wherever possible to communicate ideas and functionality to the user.

The move away from textual cues lies at the heart of the iPhone. The iPhone doesn't have pull-down menus or ribbons, and your application should not implement them. If it is well designed, its use should be intuitive. If it is not intuitive, your application is not designed for the iPhone. A user's guide for your application should not be needed if it is designed well.

One reason that pull-down menus have proliferated in many applications is that they have grown from single-use to multiple-use applications. If you look at office applications that are available, it is easy to see how they have grown from the simple, purpose-directed applications they originally were to the behemoths they have become.

Word processors are no longer word processors. They must do sophisticated layouts, be capable of including items from completely different applications, and even provide a development environment. Although this functionality creep has kept applications somewhat viable, it has made them huge and cumbersome.

Each of your iPhone applications should have one and only one purpose or function. It should be easily definable and easy for the user to grasp. By supporting Apple's standard, your application will be more readily comprehensible and yield a more pleasant user experience.

Application control is a vital component of any design. All your applications should enable the user as much control as possible. This means your application should not force the user into specific behaviors. Limiting options is frowned on in iPhone applications. To help accomplish this, your application views should be in a flat arrangement. Deep hierarchical arrangements of views puts the computer in charge and should be discouraged.

Because gestures such as touch and multitouch are the interaction methodology for the iPhone, your application should support these. Each touch location should be sized appropriately to enable the user to select it. By standard, touch locations should be about 34 pixels in width and height. If they are smaller than this because you are trying to free up screen space, the user experiences difficulty selecting screen items. A poor user experience results.

Although swipe and pinch are supported behaviors, they can be difficult for your users to discover. If you are going to include these, give visual cues about their availability. An example of a cue in an eBook application could be the inclusion of curled page corners in the visual display.

Drag-and-drop functionality is generally discouraged in the HIG because the same user interaction is typically used for scrolling or panning. However, examples of successful applications using drag and drop are easily found. Apple has even produced an overly complicated sample of how to accomplish it in JavaScript. The second part of this chapter shows you how to implement drag and drop, pinching to scale, and rotating interface elements cleanly and easily.

Table 3.1 lists each type of supported user gesture and the standard behavior that is associated with it. Following these definitions flattens the learning curve for your application. However, redefining the associated behaviors makes the learning curve steeper.

Table 3.1 **iPhone Gestures and Standardized Behaviors**

Gesture	Behavior
Tap	User interface item selection.
Drag	Scroll or pan for further viewing.

Table 3.1 **iPhone Gestures and Standardized Behaviors**

Gesture	Behavior
Flick	Quickly scroll or pan. This scrolling or panning must include continued behavior after the gesture is complete.
Swipe	Reveal hidden components, such as table view row delete buttons or additional views.
Double tap	Center and then zoom in or out.
Expanding pinch (pinch open)	Zoom in.
Contracting pinch (pinch close)	Zoom out.
Touch and hold	Display a magnified view.

The iPhone truly is an amazing device, but textual user input can be cumbersome and slow compared to standard keyboard data entry. Try to make sure that you use data selectors instead of direct input whenever possible. In hybrid applications, selectors known as pickers pop up when the user selects an HTML `<option>` tag. Using selectors in your application increases the speed with which your users control it and reduces their frustration level. Chapter 4, "GPS, Acceleration, and Other Native Functions with QuickConnect," shows you how to include standard Date/Time pickers in hybrid applications.

The standard iPhone application HIG indicates that check boxes and radio buttons should be avoided; instead, switches should be used. The Settings application ships on every iPhone and iPod touch. It uses switches heavily. Figure 3.1 shows the Safari options that are modifiable in the Settings application. For hybrid application developers, this avoidance of radio buttons and check boxes is a quandary.

The Dashcode application used to develop the UI for hybrid applications doesn't include a switch widget; however, it can be easily created. It consists of an inset-bordered box with two text elements: OFF and ON. It also includes a button.

Using the gesture events of the button, you can make it to slide right and left, yielding two states of this new switch. The *ongestureend* callback function you define for the button is used to detect and store if it is in an ON or OFF state. Figure 3.1 shows you the switches available to a user for modifying the settings of the Safari application. Make your switches look like those.

By following these basic rules of design, your application fulfills Apple's requirements for Apple Store distribution, and it fulfills user expectations of how your application should work. Violation of these concepts places your application at risk of rejection by both Apple and those who might use it.

Figure 3.1 The switches in the Settings application for Safari.

Section 2: List- and Browser-Based Interfaces

One of the basic iPhone application user interface types uses lists to organize the interface display. The HistoryExample application is one of these. In Dashcode, this interface is created two ways. The quickest of these is to use the Browser part.

The Browser part, found in the Parts Library, can be dragged directly to your application. This creates a stack of independent views. Views are the main display unit that users interact with; they are often erroneously called screens. When a Browser part is added to an application, two default views are added, but the code to switch between views is not. A header with a navigational button is also automatically added. Figure 3.2 shows Dashcode after adding the Browser part.

The button automatically added in the header does not need to be modified because the Browser part changes the text displayed by the button to be the text in the header of the previous view (if there is one). When creating an application, modify the header text, not the button text, to reflect the application's name or another appropriate display.

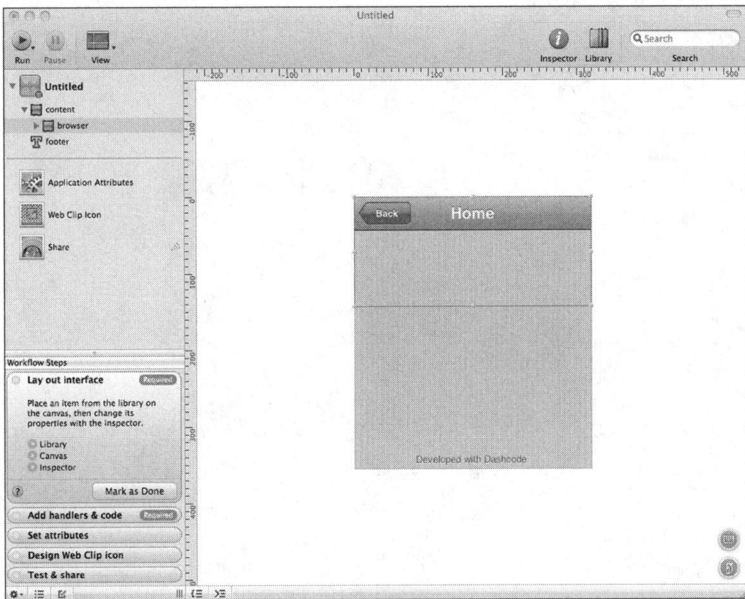

Figure 3.2 A Dashcode application after the Browser part is added

Two default named views are inserted into the project when a Browser part is added to an application. By selecting the first red inspector tab, you can see these views and rename them. Figure 3.3 shows the History sample application after the views have been renamed `mainView` and `presidentsView`. Notice there are + and – options for the Subviews list. These buttons enable you to add additional views and remove any you don't need.

All views in the application are managed in the Subviews list. Notice that even though the navigation of the application is mainView → ContinentsView → SouthAmericanView, all of the views are direct children of the stack layout. This is how applications of this type should be developed.

In both Rounded Rectangle and Edge-to-Edge lists, only the first list item is selectable in the Dashcode UI design view. This first element is used as a template for the other items in the list. Any color, content, or size changes you make to this element are applied to all the other elements in the list. This includes event listeners you assign. All elements in the lists of the History application share the same onclick event listener, the `changeView` function.

The `changeView` function is in the main.js file and is seen in the code that follows. It uses the Labels and Values entered in the attributes screen of the view's inspector to determine the new view to display. To see this function, select the view, not the first label element. In your application, this is where you add static list items, as shown in Figure 3.4.

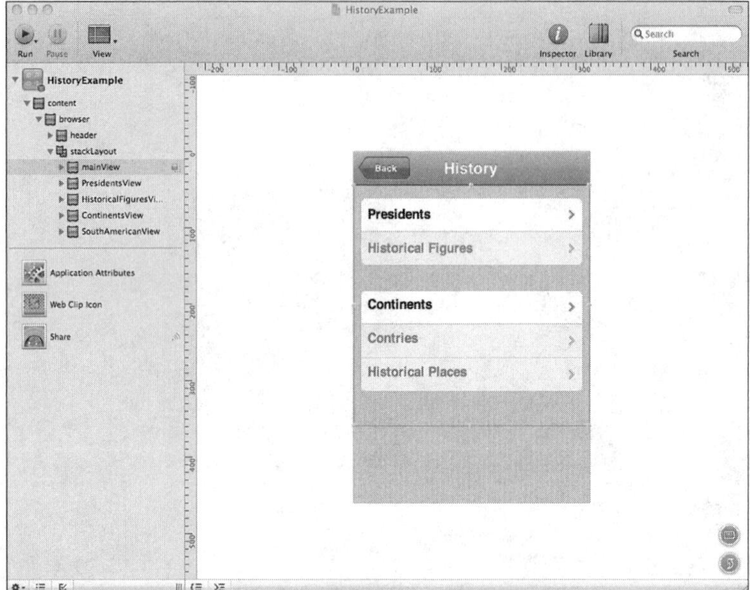

Figure 3.3 The HistoryExample application with views and two rounded rectangle lists added to the main view

```
function changeView(event)
{
    var subViewName = event.target.object.value;
    var displayName = event.target.innerText;
    var browser = document.getElementById('browser').object;
    browser.goForward(subViewName+'View', displayName);
}
```

By using these values and naming views appropriately, the `goForward` method of the `browser` object shifts the next view appropriately. This `goForward` method has two parameters. The first is the name of the view to switch to, and the second is the text to display in the header of the view. If you try to switch to a view, and the header changes but the view does not, the name of the view you are attempting to switch to is not the name of a view in your application.

When creating list- and view-based applications, be sure to organize the data correctly. If the information is contained in too many views, the user will find the navigation overly

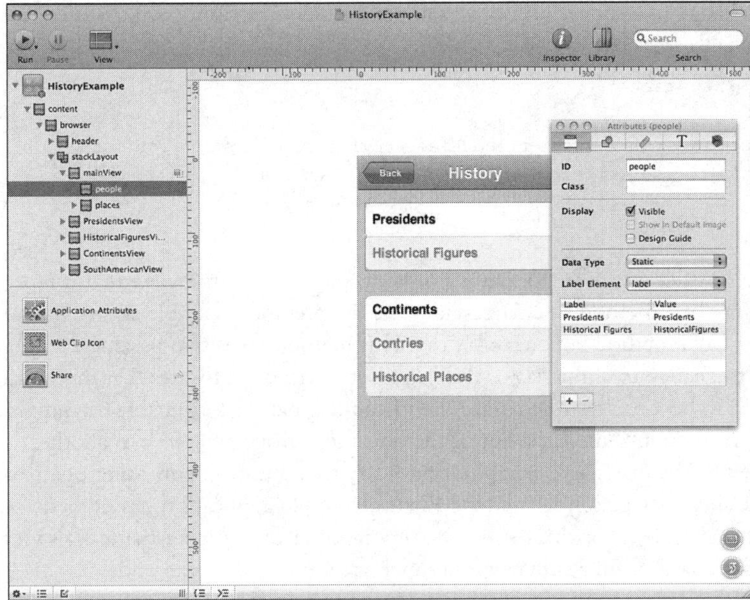

Figure 3.4 The mainView people list attributes display with two static elements added.

cumbersome. In fact, if you are not careful, you might reinvent the DOS-based navigation control from the 1970s and 1980s.

List- and view-based applications have many uses, but they are not always the most visually appealing. Sometimes something other than a list needs to be used to trigger the view changes. These applications are referred to as nonlist-based view applications.

Section 3: Nonlist-Based View Applications

Although list- and view-based applications have many uses, no rule states that all view-based applications must use lists to access the information. Other visual clues can indicate that by touching an item, additional information is displayed. The PictureExample sample application in the QuickConnectiPhone download is an example of one of these.

By indicating on the screen that something is to be touched, the user tends to touch items to see if they are active. If you choose this approach, be careful not to confuse your intended target audience members by these indicators or by what they should touch in order to control your application.

There are a couple of differences between the following code and the previous one. The first is that each of the images needs either an `onclick` or `ontouchstart` listener to trigger a change to a subview. In this example, a single function, `goSub`, is used to handle both touchable images.

```
function goSub(event)
{
    var stackLayout = document.getElementById('stackLayout').object;
    stackLayout.setCurrentView(event.target.id+'View'
                                            , false);
}
```

By giving each image an `id` that is similar to the name of the view that it represents, it is easy to use one method to change views. As the previous example shows, the stack layout object has a method `setCurrentView`. This method takes two parameters: the id of the view to change to and a flag. If the flag is set to true, it indicates that the visual change is intended to be a backward change. The id and flag parameters enable the programmer or engineer to control the behavior of the transitions from one view to another.

Unlike the HistoryExample application list type application consisting of a pre-built list, views, and a navigation header, the PictureExample application has no built-in, automated navigation bar. For this reason, the programmer or engineer that causes view changes backwards from a subview to a super-view must write the code.

Unlike the images found in the main view, the back images are intended to cause a change to the main view. Because it is awkward for a back directional transition to have the same visual behavior as a forward transition, the second parameter of the `setCurrentView` function is passed `true`. This indicates that a reverse visual transition is required.

The following `goMain` code is associated with the Back button as the `onclick` listener. It is passed *`true`* as the second argument. This causes the transition associated with the `mainView` to occur in a direction that is the reverse of the standard behavior. Thus, it is possible to make the user think a previous action is being undone.

```
function goMain(event)
{
    // Set the current view of a StackLayout
    var stackLayout = document.getElementById('stackLayout').object;
    stackLayout.setCurrentView('mainView', true);
}
```

Another difference from browser-based applications are the options for what type of transition animation to use when the views change. These are like any other piece of information given to a user. If a different transition type is used to move to one view as opposed to the others, something is different about that view. Figure 3.5 shows the list of subviews and the `goMain` function in Dashcode.

As shown in Table 3.2, you can use several types of transitions in your application. Although it is possible to use many different transactions in an application, this would be unwise.

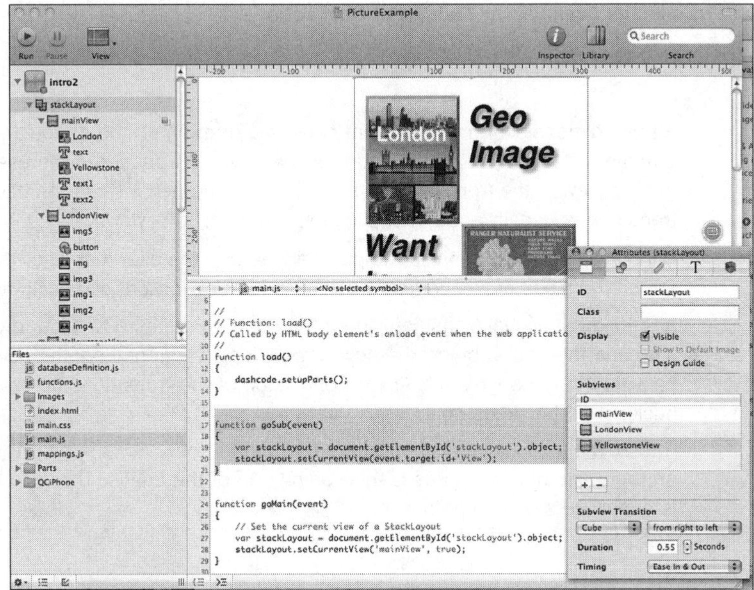

Figure 3.5 The stack layout attributes screen showing the transition options selected.

Source: http://creativecommons.org/licenses/by-sa/3.0/

Table 3.2 **Transitions Available by Default in Dashcode**

Transition Type	Behavior
push	A two-dimensional transition where the view to be displayed moves into the viewable area while the old view moves out.
dissolve	A two-dimensional transition where the view to be displayed becomes more opaque while the old view becomes more transparent. Because they overlap each other, it appears as if the old view gradually becomes the new view.
slide	A two-dimensional transition similar to push. In this case, the old view remains in place while the new view appears to slide over the top of it. This gives the user the impression of moving through a stack of views. In this case, a "backward" change, sliding off, would be drilling down into the application views, whereas a "forward" change, sliding on, would move back up the view stack.
fade	A two-dimensional transition similar to dissolve. In this case, the old view remains opaque, so that both views are visible at the completion of the transition. When this transition is done "backward," the new view becomes opaque and the original view is fully displayed. This transition is used to add new information or functionality to an existing view because both views can accept touch events.

Table 3.2 **Transitions Available by Default in Dashcode**

Transition Type	Behavior
flip	A three-dimensional transition that causes a rotation on the device's y-axis through the center of the old and the new views. It appears to the user as if the old view is the front of the application and the new view is the back. This transition is usually used in applications with only two views.
cube	A three-dimensional transition where it appears to the user that all of the views are on the sides of a cube and the cube is rotating forward and backward.
swap	A three-dimensional transition where the old view appears to slide to one side and then move below the new view. During the transition, the new view's background is transparent. At the conclusion of the transition, the new view's background becomes opaque.
revolve	A three-dimensional transition where the old and new views appear to rotate on the y-axis of the devices display along one of the edges. The visual effect is similar to a revolving door.

It appears from the Dashcode interface that the only directions available are right-to-left and left-to-right for those transitions that move. This is not the case. Top-to-bottom or bottom-to top movement is possible.

The following code is from the setup.js file from the HistoryExample. It is generated by Dashcode. As you can see, the transition types and their directions are found here for all of the views. If you want to change these, you must first turn off code generation. To do this in Dashcode, use the pull-down menu option View → Stop Code Generation.

```
var dashcodePartSpecs = {

     .

     .

     .

"stackLayout": { "creationFunction": "CreateStackLayout",
"subviewsTransitions": [{ "direction": "right-left", "duration": "",
"timing": "ease-in-out", "type": "push" }, { "direction": "right-left",
"duration": "", "timing": "ease-in-out", "type": "push" }, {
"direction": "right-left", "duration": "", "timing": "ease-in-out",
"type": "push" }, { "direction": "right-left", "duration": "",
"timing": "ease-in-out", "type": "push" }, { "direction": "right-left",
"duration": "", "timing": "ease-in-out", "type": "push" }] }

     .

     .

     .

};
```

Because Dashcode generates a great deal of code for you and replaces the contents of the setup.js file regularly, you should not modify this file until your application is complete. It is easiest to modify this file after it is placed in the Xcode QuickConnectiPhone template because Dashcode is no longer involved. Because it is not involved, it cannot overwrite any changes you make.

The previous code contains the declaration of four JavaScript objects. Each object begins with a `{` character, ends with `},` and contains a `direction`, `duration`, `timing`, and `type` attribute. One of these objects, the second, is bold to help you distinguish it from the others.

Each these anonymous objects defines the behavior of a transition from one view to another. The bold object code declares a transition of push type, as described in Table 3.2. It pushes in from the left to the right in an ease-in- out manner. Ease-in- out means that it gradually speeds up and slows down as the transition is completed.

Other timing options are ease-in, ease-out, and the default. The default is constant speed timing and is used when the transition definition object's `timing` attribute is not set.

As mentioned earlier, other options for transition direction exist and are top-bottom and bottom-top. These do not work for all transition types. The slide and push transitions accept these directions, but none of the others.

If you choose to make modifications to these object declarations, be aware that they can cause problems if your application is more complex. It seems that Apple left out the capability to choose some transition definition options because they cause the webkit engine used in Safari and the UIWebView object found in hybrid applications to misbehave.

Section 4: Immersion Applications

Immersion type applications are a dramatic departure from using views for grouping information display and control. The most common form these applications take is in games, but current examples of iPhone medical applications also apply this approach. The idea is that user interaction with the application should be natural, flowing, and, whenever possible, within one view.

Although this approach in its extreme form is used in games, it can also be used in other ways. For example, the medical imaging applications use this approach and the touch capability of the iPhone to dramatically change the way doctors interact with medical images.

There is no reason innovative application engineers cannot use this same approach in business or science. One reason that poor business decisions are made is that it is difficult to display related and complicated pieces of information with the simple charts and graphs used today. To look at data in a different way, a new way of displaying data must be used.

If data can be displayed visually in a nonlinear form encompassing the entire screen, related data can be used as an overlay to it in order to find relationships. A simple form of this approach is the map application's capability to show not only a route from one location to another, but to also show traffic density on and near the route. Thus, two pieces of information are overlaid so the user can find a useful pattern.

This book doesn't pretend to offer an approach for how data can be manipulated for display. It simply suggests that it can be done and is being done. The example in this section is a game.

The DollarStash game is a variation of Apple's Leaves example web application. In that application, a series of images are inserted into a page that gradually fall to the bottom of the screen, twisting and turning as they fall. To make this into a game, the leaves were changed to icons that represent money.

As the user touches a bill the amount of money in his account increases by one. If a bill fades completely away before it is touched, the player's account amount is decreased by one. Groups of bills are displayed in waves at the top of the screen. Each wave contains one more bill than the previous wave. When the player's balance drops below zero, the game ends. Figure 3.6 shows the game in play. Although this game was put together quickly, it dramatically points out one of the limitations of this type of application in a hybrid environment.

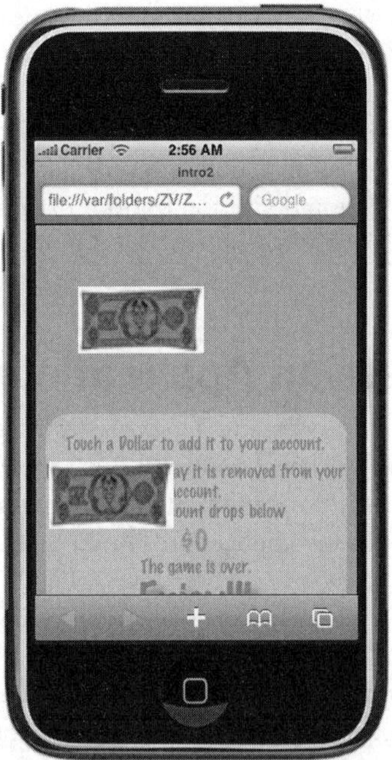

Figure 3.6 The DollarStash game in progress

The UIWebView uses the same WebKit engine as Safari and other applications to render the screen. This engine and others like it have made significant strides in recent years. One common problem they have is that when the CPU becomes taxed, user interface events such as clicks and touches get ignored. As you play the DollarStash game on your device, not the simulator, you will find that this is the case.

As the number of bills increases, the number of touches that are missed by the engine also increases. To subject your user to such annoyance violates a basic rule of user interface design mentioned in the first section of this chapter: rapid response to user input.

The user interaction intensive portions of these types of applications are best written in Objective-C. That does not mean applications cannot use a UIWebView for complex textual layout and simple image display. It does mean that until iPhone's and iPod touch's CPUs get a dramatic speed increase, using the native Cascading Style Sheet (CSS) transforms and animations for complex game creation is not viable.

Knowing the limitations of your device can lead you in the direction of a better design. Although highly CPU-intensive games are not viable in hybrid applications, using the CSS transforms and animations to accomplish drag-and-drop, scaling, and rotation behaviors is viable when used on one interface element at a time.

Section 5: Creating and Using Custom CSS Transforms

This section shows you how to create drag-and-drop, scale, and rotate capabilities using the new CSS transforms built into the WebKit engine used by Safari and the UIWebView. To learn more about CSS transitions, transforms, and animations, see Apple's user guide found at http://developer.apple.com/documentation/InternetWeb/Conceptual/SafariVisualAffectsProgGuide/Introduction/chapter_1_1.html#//apple_ref/doc/uid/TP40008032-CH1-SW1.

Several implementations of drag-and-drop type behavior are available for download and are written in JavaScript. These implementations are great for cross-browser use on desktop machines. They fail on the iPhone and iPod touch because the implementations are CPU-intensive. However, a good alternative is the use of CSS transforms.

WebKit, the engine used in Safari and the UIWebView found in hybrid applications, includes the capability to define transitions in CSS. These transitions are hardware-accelerated, making them more efficient than making changes using JavaScript as other libraries do.

A simple example is to shift the position of an HTML div down the screen. To do this using traditional JavaScript, you need to modify the top attribute of the div's style. Assume that a div is assigned a CSS class that sets the top attribute to 50 pixels from the top of the page. A shift down an additional 50 pixels is accomplished by setting the same attribute to 100 pixels, as seen in the following:

```
adiv.style.top =  '100px';
```

This declaration is interpreted as a JavaScript command and is executed by the engine at the same speed and using the same CPU resources as any other JavaScript command. The CSS transform alternative is done differently.

Using CSS transforms to accomplish a 50-pixel change in location from the original declared position also requires the use of the div's style declaration. However, in this case, a completely different attribute is used.

One of the new attributes added to CSS classes, and therefore, the style attribute of an Element object in JavaScript, is `webKitTransform`. This attribute, when set correctly, causes hardware-accelerated native functions to be called. It is not interpreted as JavaScript. Because of this, any CSS attribute change defined is executed much faster than if you used the previous JavaScript example.

The transform example shown here also requires only one line of code:

```
adiv.style.webKitTransform = 'translateY(50px)';
```

At first glance, the transform attribute appears to be a function pointer like `onclick`, `ontouch`, and other event listeners. In fact, it is not.

The major difference between `webKitTransform` and the listeners is that no JavaScript function declared inline or as a Window function is assigned. A string describing which standard function is to be called and its parameters are assigned instead. This string is then parsed by the WebKit engine in a portion of its code distinct from where JavaScript is interpreted.

Also notice that the translation amount declared is relative to the original location of the div. To shift an Element down an additional 50 pixels, the parameter passed to `translateY` is `50px`. It is also important to understand that the original location definition has not been changed. The div is still assigned the original `top` value of 50px. Only the location at which it is rendered has changed. If you query the object after the translation has occurred and print out the `top` value, it would still be 50px, not 100px.

The Drag sample application shows how to make a div move on the screen using a translate function. To accomplish this, the div that is to be dragged is assigned listeners for the `ontouchstart`, `ontouchchange`, and `ontouchend` events.

Touch events differ from the standard `onclick`, `onmousedown`, `onmousemove`, and `onmouseup` events used in traditional desktop drag-and-drop JavaScript implementations. Because a touch might consist of two or more individual touches, such as when a user places two or three fingers on the screen, a touch event needs to contain information about each touch.

Each of the individual touches and its information is stored in an array that is an attribute of an event object that is called `targetTouches`. This array is sized according to the number of fingers the user has applied to the element found on the screen of the device. Thus, if one finger is applied, the array has a size of one. For two fingers, it has a size of two.

Each object stored in the array is of type Touch and has many of the attributes usually associated with a mouse event in JavaScript. Table 3.3 describes each of these attributes.

The drag-and-drop implementation shown here uses the clientX and clientY attributes because there is no scrolling allowed in the sample application. If there was, the pageX and pageY attributes would be used.

Table 3.3 **Attributes of the Touch Class**

Attribute	Description
pageX	The offset in the horizontal direction from the left side of the entire document including horizontal scrolling information
pageY	The offset in the vertical direction from the top of the entire document including vertical scrolling information
screenX	The offset in the horizontal direction from the left side of the device's screen
screenY	The offset in the vertical direction from the top of the device's screen
clientX	The offset in the horizontal direction from the left side of the application window
clientY	The offset in the vertical direction from the top of the application window
target	The DOM object representing the HTML element that was touched

One problem encountered when implementing drag-and-drop is "hopping" elements that occur when dragging begins. This hopping occurs because the user has selected the object by touching it somewhere in its boundaries, and yet, the translation of the device is applied to the upper, left-hand corner. If nothing is done to handle this mismatch, the upper, left-hand corner of the object being dragged "hops" to the location of the user's finger when dragging begins.

Obviously the user sees this as abnormal. For example, if the user selects the center of the object to start the drag, he would reasonably expect his finger to stay in the center of the object as he drags it. It would be disconcerting if it did not stay in the center. Figure 3.7 shows a the Drag sample application running.

To remedy this, the drag sample application assigns the `setStartLocation` function to the `ontouchstart` JavaScript event handler. This function, found in the following code and the main.js file of the example, retrieves and stores the location of the original touch event, in pixels, in the x and y directions from the top, left corner of the application window.

```
function setStartLocation(event)
{
        var element = event.target;
        element.offsetX = event.targetTouches[0].clientX;
        element.offsetY = event.targetTouches[0].clientY;
}
```

By storing this distance as the `offsetX` and `offsetY` attributes of the element touched, it can later be used when the element is dragged to stop the hopping from happening. The actual moving of the element happens not in the `setStartLocation` function but in the `drag` function that is assigned as the `ontouchchange` event listener. The `drag` function is also found in the main.js file.

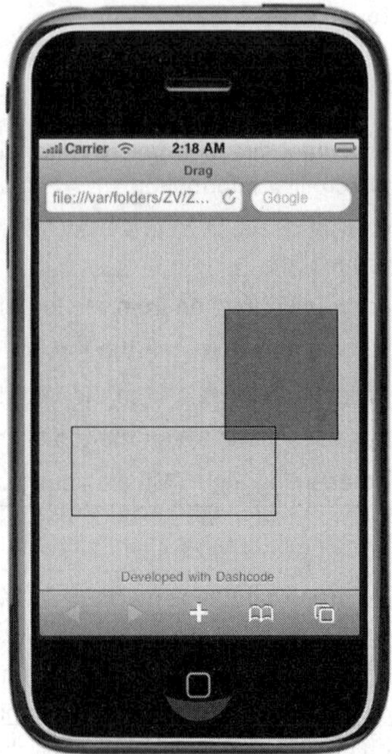

Figure 3.7 The Drag sample application after the green div has been moved

Line 3 in the drag function, as shown in the following code, is vital to any drag-and-drop implementation for the iPhone and iPod touch. Normally, when a touch change event is triggered, the Safari browser or UIWebView scrolls. To turn off this behavior, the event must be informed not to trigger its standard behavior. This is done by calling the event's `preventDefault` method. If this method is called in an `ontouchchange` listener, the view will not scroll when a finger is moved within the element to which the listener is assigned.

Being free from the default scroll behavior enables you to change the location at which the element is rendered using webkitTransform. To do this, the current touches location needs to be found and compared with the original touch location stored in the `setStartLocation` function.

```
1 function drag(event)
2 {
3     event.preventDefault();
4     var element = event.target;
5     element.x = event.targetTouches[0].clientX
6                          - event.target.offsetX;
```

```
7    element.y = event.targetTouches[0].clientY
8                          - event.target.offsetY;
9    if(element.lastX || element.lastY){
10       element.x += element.lastX;
11       element.y += element.lastY;
12    }
13    element.style.webkitTransform = 'translate('
14                   + element.x + 'px, '
15                   + element.y + 'px)';
16 }
```

The code found in lines 5–8 in the previous code calculates the amount that the rendering of the element needs offset by in both the x and y directions. These offsets, in pixels, are stored in the x and y attributes of the current element for later use and then used on lines 13–15 to accomplish the display change using the `translate` function described earlier.

Because it is possible that this drag is not the first to be done by the user for an element, it is necessary to keep track of and use the offsets that were applied previously. These offsets are applied in lines 9–11 in the previous code and are stored in the `done` method that follows. This method is assigned as the `ontouchend` listener.

```
function done(event)
{
    var element = event.target;
    element.lastX = element.x;
    element.lastY = element.y;
}
```

The `done` method exists for one reason only: to store the current offset amount for reuse should the user drag the element again. It does this by storing the element's current `x` and `y` attributes in its `lastX` and `lastY` attributes. By doing this, it ensures that they are available when each of the `ontouchchange` events is fired as the user moves his finger on the screen.

By adding these three methods as listeners to elements of your user interface, they can be dragged by the user in a simple fashion. In the next section, you learn how to create and use an easier-to-use, less naïve module for drag-and-drop.

In addition to drag–and-drop, iPhone applications often need the capability to scale and rotate elements of the interface. These elements may be divs, buttons, images, or any other organizational or visual element. Interestingly enough, the code required to accomplish this is much smaller than drag-and-drop. It is obvious that Apple intends engineers and developers to include this behavior in their applications.

The gestures sample application shows how scaling and rotating can be easily done. Instead of touches, it uses gestures. Gestures differ from touches in that they always assume more than one finger is being used and include user behaviors such as pinch.

To represent these gestures, a `GestureEvent` is passed to any gesture-listening function. Because they represent gestures, they do not include location information like a `TouchEvent`. They do include three important pieces of information, as seen in Table 3.4.

Table 3.4 **The Important Attributes of the GestureEvent**

Attribute	Description
scale	A positive or negative double value representing the change in distance between two fingers used in a gesture. Negative values indicate that the fingers have crossed. This attribute is used in pinch-gesture handling.
rotation	A positive or negative double value measured in degrees that represents the rotational difference between the locations of two fingers used in a gesture and a vertical line. This attribute is used in rotation-gesture handling.
target	The DOM object representing the HTML element in which the gesture occurred.

The gestures example application uses these three events to scale and rotate a div. This is accomplished adding an `ongesturechange` event handler called `changeIt` to the div itself. This addition of event handlers is done using the Behaviors tab of the inspector window. The code for this method is

```
function changeIt(event)
{
        event.preventDefault();
        var element = event.target;

        element.style.webkitTransform=
                        'rotateZ('+event.rotation
                        +'deg) scale('+event.scale+')';
}
```

Notice that just as in the Drag example application that the event's default behavior must be turned off to prevent scrolling. Unlike the Drag application, the rotation and scaling information is not stored. Storage of the rotation information is not required because it is relative to a baseline, not the object being transformed.

Scaling information should be stored so it can be used during the next gesture because it is relative to the element being transformed and has a cumulative effect. Storage of the scaling information has been left out of the gestures example application and the previous code to show you the scaling error the user of an application will see if it is not stored. The next section shows you how to store and reuse scaling information.

Notice that there are two functions used in the string that defines the webkitTransform. This enables you to rotate and scale the div in one call. They can be broken up and used conditionally.

Three rotate functions are available to you as you create your application. Each of them rotates the element of your choice around one of the axes of your phone. The x-axis is horizontal, the y-axis is vertical, and the z-axis extends out of the screen. When the previous code specifies `rotateZ`, it indicates that the div should rotate on the x-y plane of the device as seen in Figure 3.8.

Figure 3.8 Application of the rotateZ function of webkitTransform

You can easily change the rotation so that the div rotates differently. If you use the `rotateY` in the example, the div rotates around the y-axis and appears to get narrower before displaying the back of the div. If you change the rotation to `rotateX`, the div rotates around the x-axis and appears to get shorter before displaying the back side of the div.

You might consider creating a cover flow implementation using rotation. At the time of writing this book, this implementation was unadvisable. Because of the number of transforms required to get cover flow like behavior any implementation the CPU of the iPhone or iPod touch becomes over-taxed and the user experience is poor.

Now that you have seen naïve implementations of drag-and-drop, scaling, and rotating, it is possible to understand a sophisticated module that implements these.

Section 6: Using and Creating a Drag-and-Drop/Scale/Rotate Module

Modules, as described in Chapter 2, "JavaScript Modularity and iPhone Applications," are complete and independent in their functionalities. In other words, they are said to be loosely coupled to the rest of the code in an application and have tight cohesion. Well designed modules always come with an API. The API that is implemented in this section is shown in Table 3.5.

Table 3.5 **The Drag-and-Drop Scale Rotation API**

Function	Parameter	Description
`makeDraggable`	`element` (required)—The DOM element that is to be dragged. `startDragCmd` (optional)—A command that is mapped to Control Functions that are called at the end of the `ontouchstart` event. `dragCmd` (optional)—A command that is mapped to Control Functions that are called at the end of all `ontouchmove` events. `dropCmd` (optional)—A command that is mapped to Control Functions that are called at the end of the `ontouchend` event.	This function sets up the event listeners for the element passed in, so that the user can drag it.
`makeChangeable`	`element` (required)—The DOM element that is scaled and rotated. `startChangeCmd` (optional)—A command that is mapped to Control Functions that are called at the end of the `ongesturestart` event. `dragCmd` (optional)—A command that is mapped to Control Functions that are called at the end of all `ongesturechange` events. `doneChangeCmd` (optional)—A command that is mapped to Control Functions that are called at the end of the `ongestureend` event.	This function sets up the event listeners for the element passed in, so that the user can be scaled and rotate it around the z-axis.

These two functions are all your code needs to call to give your user drag-and-drop capability and scaling and rotation (see Figure 3.9). The dragAndGesture example application is found in the Examples directory. It can be downloaded from https://sourceforge.net/project/showfiles.php?group_id=213586 as part of QuickConnect-iPhone. The functions are found in the QCUtilities.js file of the framework in the same download.

Figure 3.9 The dragAndGesture example application runs with one element rotated and moved.

The load function in the main.js file and seen in the following code shows how these functions are used with elements in a user interface.

```
function load()
{
    .
    .
    .

      var anElement = document.getElementById('button');
      makeDraggable(anElement);
      makeChangeable(anElement);
```

```
    anElement = document.getElementById('imageBox');
    makeDraggable(anElement);
    makeChangeable(anElement);

    anElement = document.getElementById('box');
    makeDraggable(anElement);
    makeChangeable(anElement);

    anElement = document.getElementById('stuff');
    makeDraggable(anElement);
}
```

In the previous example, three different elements of the UI are changed so they can be dragged, scaled, and rotated, and the fourth can be dragged only. Notice that after getting a reference to the UI element, it is passed to the appropriate function or functions of the API. This is all that is required to make your UI elements active.

The naïve implementations of drag-and-drop, scale, and rotate seen earlier in this section act independently of each other. As you can see, the previous example indicates that they should be able to act in concert. To do this, they need to know the effect, if any, that the other implementations have had on the element. This change begins in the `makeDraggable` and `makeChangeable` functions.

The `makeDraggable` API function handles the setup and management of the `ontouchstart` event listener and any commands that might have been sent for post-event handling.

```
function makeDraggable(anElement, startDragCmd
                                , dragCmd, dropCmd){
    anElement.ontouchstart = prepareDrag;
    anElement.isDraggable = true;
    if(startDragCmd){
        anElement.startDragCmd = startDragCmd;
    }
    if(dragCmd){
        anElement.dragCmd = dragCmd;
    }
    if(dropCmd){
        anElement.dropCmd = dropCmd;
    }
}
```

Notice that the element's `isDraggable` attribute is set to true. This is the first piece of information that has been stored to enable the two functionalities to work together. Also notice that only one touch listener, `ontouchstart`, is set in this function. The reason behind this is to ignore touches when an element is scaled or rotated; this is discussed later in this section.

The makeChangeable function is similar. It sets the gesture listeners, sets the isChangeable attribute to true, and stores post-event commands for later use. Unlike the makeDraggable function, this function sets the gesture listeners. This is because when touch events are fired because of the single touches of dragging, no gesture events are fired. If an element is draggable and dragging happens, touch events are fired and acted on. If an element is changeable and a gesture happens, both touch and gesture events are fired, the touch events are ignored, and the gesture events are acted on.

```
function makeChangeable(anElement, startChangeCmd,
                            changeCmd, doneChangeCmd){
      anElement.ongesturestart = prepareGesture;
      anElement.ongesturechange = changeIt;
      anElement.ongestureend = gestureDone;
      anElement.isChangeable = true;
      anElement.oldRotation = 0;
      anElement.oldScale = 1;
      anElement.startChangeCmd = startChangeCmd;
      anElement.changeCmd = changeCmd;
      anElement.doneChangeCmd = doneChangeCmd;
}
```

Two other pieces of information are initialized in the makeChangeable method. These are accumulators for scale and rotation called oldScale and oldRotation, respectively.

When the gestures example application is used, each time the element is rotated or scaled, it instantly resizes itself back to its original size. This is because no automatic storage of the scaling already done is available to application. The oldScale attribute of the element is used to solve this problem.

The oldScale attribute is initialized to 1 because scaling is a multiplier that is applied to the width and height of an element; this is discussed later in this section. If the amount to be scaled is between 0 inclusive and 1 exclusive, it gets smaller. If the scaling amount is 1, the element remains unchanged and for any other condition it gets larger.

When an element has been scaled once, the amount it is scaled must be used in conjunction with the new scaling amount to correctly size the element. For example, if the first time an element is scaled, it doubled in size, the oldScale value would be set to 2. If the user pinches the element to make it 90 percent of its size, the current scaling value would be 2 * .9, which equals 1.8. If the oldScale value is not retained, the size would instantly become .9 and not match the intent of the user who performed the pinch.

Previously, the prepareDrag function was assigned to the ontouchstart event listener. This function, as shown in the following code, contains several interesting pieces of functionality. The first functionality is the storage of an array of Touch objects, described earlier in this section. This is done to enable the gesture event-listening functions access to the specific touch information. For example, touch events might need to know how many touches cause the gesture event. That is not available from within the events passed to gesture listeners.

```
1 function prepareDrag(event){
2     stopDefault(event);
3     this.touches = event.targetTouches;
4     var self = this;
5     this.timeOut = setTimeout(function(){
6         if(self.changing){
7         return;
8         }
9         self.dragging = true;
10         self.ontouchmove = dragIt;
11         self.ontouchend = dragDone;
12         self.offsetX = event.targetTouches[0].clientX;
13         self.offsetY = event.targetTouches[0].clientY;
14         self.oldZIndex = self.style.zIndex;
15         self.style.zIndex = 50;
16         if(self.startDragCmd){
17         var params = new Array();
18         params.push(event);
19         params.push(self);
20         handleRequest(self.startDragCmd, params);
21     }
22  }, 75);
23 }
```

Another item of interest in the previous code appears on line 5. Instead of instantly storing the initial location of the touch as the `offsetX` and `offsetY` attributes of the element being dragged, a timer is used to delay setting these and other values. This is done because the `prepareDrag` function might have been called as the result of the user performing a gesture.

Touch events triggered because gestures always occur prior to the gesture events being triggered. If the event passed to `prepareDrag` truly is the result of a gesture, the `ontouchmove` and `ontouchend` event listeners must not be set or they would be called as the gesture changes and ends. If these listeners were called, they would execute dragging behavior and cause the gesture behavior to malfunction.

The timer created needs to delay long enough to allow the gesture listener function `prepareGesture` to be called because it updates the `changing` attribute of the element being changed.

Line 22 indicates that the delay should be 75 milliseconds. This gives sufficient time for the gesture listener to be called and executed, if a gesture occurs, but it is short enough not to annoy the user if a drag is what occurs. Should this delay time be too long, the user can readily drag his finger off the element before the element moves. The last item of interest is the population of a `params` array and the call to `handleRequest`.

The `handleRequest` function call on line 20 enables you to create callout functions that execute each time a touch event is a drag. These callout functions are defined using `mapCommandTo*` functions in the mapping file, as described in Chapter 2. You can call any number of Business Control Functions (BCF) and View Control Functions (VCF) when a drag starts. You might want, for example, to use this to remove the element from its parent, change its background color or borders, or for another purpose.

Because it is unknown how or if you will use these callout functions, certain information is included in the `param` array that is passed. This array, as shown in the previous code, includes the element that is dragged and the dragging event. It is unknown whether you need these in callout functions you might create, but they are added for your convenience.

As a user moves his finger across the screen, the `ontouchmove` event listener `dragIt` is called repeatedly. The purpose of this function, like the `drag` function in the Drag example application, is to move the element in conjunction with the movement of the user's finger. However, you can see the application of the information stored previously in the gesture listener functions and in `prepareDrag`.

Because a transform is used to do both the drag-and-drop, when a drag is done, any rotational and scaling that has been done previously must be applied in addition to the translation. This is due to the fact that the style's `webkitTransform` is reset each time it is used. If rotation and scaling information is not included in the transform string, the element would assume its original size and orientation as soon as it was dragged.

A transform string that causes a translation, a rotation, and scaling when fully assembled contains multiple functions and looks like this:

```
"translate(-1px, 5px) rotateZ(21deg) scale(0.9)"
```

This line of code moves the element 1 pixel to the left and 5 pixels down. It then rotates the element around its z-axis. Then it makes the element 90 percent of the original size.

The order of the function descriptions is important. If the rotation is included in the string to the left of the translation, the rotation happens first and the translation is done at an angle to the x- and y-axis instead of along them. This would cause faulty drag-and-drop behavior because the element that is dragged would move at an angle to the movement of the user's finger instead of with it.

The code that assembles the string for the module is found on lines 13–25. These lines consist of concatenating a substring that is added to a string that contains the translate function declaration.

```
1 function dragIt(event){
2     stopDefault(event);
3
4     this.x = event.targetTouches[0].clientX - this.offsetX;
5     this.y = event.targetTouches[0].clientY - this.offsetY;
6
7     if(this.lastX || this.lastY){
8         this.x += this.lastX;
9         this.y += this.lastY;
10     }
11     this.style.webkitTransformOriginX = '50%';
12     this.style.webkitTransformOriginY = '50%';
13     var modStringFragment = '';
```

```
14      if(this.isChangeable){
15          if(this.rotation){
16              modStringFragment +=
17                          ' rotateZ('+this.oldRotation+'deg)';
18          }
19          if(this.oldScale){
20              modStringFragment +=
21                          ' scale('+this.oldScale+')';
22          }
23      }
24      var modString = 'translate(' + this.x + 'px, '
25                          + this.y + 'px)'+modStringFragment;
26
27      this.style.webkitTransform = modString;
28      if(this.dragCmd){
29          var params = new Array();
30          params.push(event);
31          params.push(this);
32          handleRequest(this.dragCmd, params);
33      }
34 }
```

Another item of importance happens on lines 11 and 12. The `webkitTransformOriginX` and `webkitTransformOriginY` attributes are set to their default values. This must be done if there is any rotation or scaling, as you see later in this section. If it is not done, when the user drags an element, it hops and the user's finger is not over the same spot on the element that it originally touched.

When the user lifts a finger from the device screen, an `ontouchend` event is fired and the `dragDone` listener function is called. The purpose of this function, as shown in the following code and found in QCUtilities.js, is to reset some of the attributes of the element to their original values and store other information for later use.

```
function dragDone(event){
    this.dragging = false;
    this.ontouchmove = null;
    this.ontouchend = null;
    this.lastX = this.x;
    this.lastY = this.y;
    this.style.zIndex = this.oldZIndex;

    if(this.dropCmd){
        var params = new Array();
        params.push(event);
        params.push(this);
        handleRequest(this.dropCmd, params);
    }
}
```

In this function, the `ontouchmove` and `ontouchend` listeners reset to their cleared states, so as not to interfere with the gesture handling, as was discussed earlier. The current `x` and `y` values of the event are stored, and a command is handled if one was set.

Having seen the full flow of the sophisticated drag-and-drop methods, the corresponding gesture-handling is more fully understandable. Just as the gesture handling can affect the code required to do drag-and-drop, drag-and-drop handling can affect the code required to do scaling and rotation.

The `prepareGesture` function, seen in the following code and found in the QCUtilities.js file, is simpler than the `prepareDrag` function discussed earlier in this section. It sets a few attributes, but it does not need to delay as the other prepare function does. The lack of need for delay in this function is discussed earlier in this section.

```
function prepareGesture(event){
    stopDefault(event);
    this.changing = true;
    this.oldZIndex = this.style.zIndex;
    this.style.zIndex = 50;

    if(this.startChangeCmd){
        var params = new Array();
        params.push(event);
        params.push(this);
        handleRequest(this.startChangeCmd, params);
    }
}
```

As with all the gesture event-handling functions, this one instructs the framework to handle a command by calling the `handleRequest` function. You can execute any number of callout functions after any gesture event listener has completed. See Chapter 2 for a discussion of how to map commands to functions.

As the user moves his fingers across the screen, an `ongesturechange` event fires repeatedly causing the `changeIt` function, shown in the following code and in the QCUtilities.js file, to be called. This function is responsible for scaling and rotating the element based on the user's interaction with the device.

```
"rotateZ(21deg) scale(0.9) translate(-1px, 5px)"
```

Note that it is possible to do a finger gesture in two or more different elements. This is usually an accident on the user's part, and therefore, lines 5–8 exist to stop the elements from reacting when they are touched.

It is also possible for the user to pinch, which can cause an element to become too small for two fingers. If this were allowed, the user couldn't resize the element, making the element unable to be modified. Lines 14–19 stop the user from accidentally making an element too small to scale up.

As discussed earlier, the order of function declarations in the transform string is important. To successfully rotate and scale an element, translation must occur, but it must be declared at the end of the string.

If translation happens first when the user attempts to rotate an element, the element would gradually move during the rotation. If no translation is included, the element rotates around its original top, left corner, as defined in its assigned CSS class. In either case, this is an unacceptable behavior.

```
function changeIt(event){
    stopDefault(event);
    //the user may have only put
    //one finger inside of the target.
    if(this.dragging
            || (this.touches && this.touches.length < 2)){
        return;
    }

     this.rotation = event.rotation;
     var rotationValue = this.rotation + this.oldRotation;
     var scaleValue = event.scale * this.oldScale;
     //don't let it get to small to allow two touches
     if(this.offsetWidth * scaleValue < 150){
         scaleValue = 150/this.offsetWidth;
     }
     else if(this.offsetHeight * scaleValue < 150){
         scaleValue = 150/this.offsetHeight;
     }
     this.scale = scaleValue;

     var modString = 'rotateZ('+rotationValue+
                         'deg) scale('+scaleValue+')';
     if(this.lastX || this.lastY){
         modString += ' translate(' + this.lastX + 'px, '
                        + this.lastY + 'px)';
         //update the center of rotation
         this.xCenterOffset = 50
                         + (this.lastX/this.offsetWidth)
                         * 100;
         this.yCenterOffset = 50
                         + (this.lastY/this.offsetHeight)
                         * 100;

         this.style.webkitTransformOriginX =
                          (this.xCenterOffset)+'%';
         this.style.webkitTransformOriginY =
                         this.yCenterOffset)+'%';
```

```
39     }
40     this.style.webkitTransform = modString;
41
42     if(this.changeCmd){
43         var params = new Array();
44         params.push(event);
45         params.push(this);
46         handleRequest(this.changeCmd, params);
47     }
48 }
```

Lines 22–39 create the transform string and set the `webkitTransformOrigin` values so that scaling and rotation can happen based on the visual center of the element being changed. The origin changes seen in the previous code are what made it necessary to reset them in the `dragIt` method discussed earlier. The transform origin is set as the middle of the element based on its current offset from its original location.

When the user lifts his fingers, an `ongestureend` event is fired, and the `gestureDone` event handler, seen below, is called. It is like the `dragDone` method with one major exception; it also has a timer like the `prepareDrag` function.

```
1 function gestureDone(event){
2     this.style.zIndex = this.oldZIndex;
3     //the user may not have done a rotation.
4     //if they did not rotation is undefined
5     if(this.rotation){
6         this.oldRotation += this.rotation;
7     }
8     //the user may not have done a pinch.
9     //if they did not scale is undefined
10     if(this.scale){
11         this.oldScale = this.scale;
12     }
13
14     if(this.doneChangeCmd){
15         var params = new Array();
16         params.push(event);
17         params.push(this);
18         handleRequest(this.doneChangeCmd, params);
19     }
20     var self = this;
21     this.timeOut = setTimeout(function(){
22         self.changing = false;
23         },75);
24 }
```

This timer, found on lines 21–23, has a similar reason for existence as did the one in `prepareDrag`. When the `ongestureend` event fires, some touch events have not been handled yet. If the `changing` attribute of the element is immediately set to false (see line 22), then based on the code in `prepareDrag` seen earlier, the event listeners for dragging are activated.

If these drag listeners are activated for a scale or rotate gesture, the element hops erratically on the screen and the user experience is negatively impacted.

Although the drag-and-drop, scale, and rotate behaviors must know about each other, their behaviors must be strictly segregated. If they are not, confusing, random application behavior occurs. The code in this section and in the QCUtilities.js file provides you with a usable, out-of-the-box implementation of drag-and-drop, scale, and rotation behaviors.

Summary

From the user's point of view, your application's interface is your application. A poor user interface design, such as in the DollarStash game anti-example, can sink your application before it gets a chance to be improved or corrected. As described in this chapter, wise interface design takes advantage of three basic principles:

- Don't surprise the user. Use commonly known interaction behaviors.
- Make the interface intuitive. The user shouldn't need to read about how to use the application.
- Don't make demands on your devices that they cannot handle. You have limited CPU and memory resources. Use them wisely.

If you follow these basic rules and Apple's HIG, your application has a much better chance of success. Although these rules may seem strict, they still allow for creativity, as shown with the drag-and-drop, scale, and rotate module.

This module, if created and used wisely, can dramatically improve the user experience of your application because it is based on the inherent multitouch capability of the iPhone and iPod touch devices and Apple's HIG.

4

GPS, Acceleration, and Other Native Functions with QuickConnect

The iPhone has many unique capabilities that you can use in your applications. These capabilities include vibrating the phone, playing system sounds, accessing the accelerometer, and using GPS location information. It is also possible to write debug messages to the Xcode console when you write your application. Accessing these capabilities is not limited to Objective-C applications. Your hybrid applications can do these things from within JavaScript. The first section of this chapter explains how to use these and other native iPhone functionalities with the QuickConnect JavaScript API. The second section shows the Objective-C code underlying the QuickConnect JavaScript Library.

Section 1: JavaScript Device Activation

The iPhone is a game-changing device. One reason for this is that access to hardware such as the accelerometer that is available to people creating applications. These native iPhone functions enable you to create innovative applications. You decide how your application should react to a change in the acceleration or GPS location. You decide when the phone vibrates or plays some sort of audio.

The QuickConnectiPhone com.js file has a function that enables you to access this behavior in a simple, easy-to-use manner. The `makeCall` function is used in your application to make requests of the phone. To use `makeCall`, you need to pass two parameters. The first is a command string and the second is a string version of any parameters that might be needed to execute the command. Table 4.1 lists each standard command, the parameters required for it, and the behavior of the phone when it acts on the command.

Table 4.1 **MakeCall Commands API**

Command String	Message String	Behavior
logMessage	Any information to be logged in the Xcode terminal.	The message appears in the Xcode terminal when the code runs.
rec	A JSON string of a JavaScript array containing the name of the audio file to create as the first element. The second element of the array is either `start` or `stop` depending on if your desire is to start or stop recording audio data.	A caf audio file with the name defined in the message string is created.
play	A JSON string of a JavaScript array containing the name of the audio file to be played as the first element. The second element of the array is either `start` or `stop` depending on if your desire is to start or stop playing the audio file.	The caf audio file, if it exists, is played through the speakers of the device or the headphones.
loc	None	The Core Location behavior of the device is triggered and the latitude, longitude, and altitude information are passed back to your JavaScript application.
playSound	–1	The device vibrates.
playSound	0	The laser audio file is played.
showDate	DateTime	The native date and time picker is displayed.
showDate	Date	The native date picker is displayed.

The DeviceCatalog sample application includes a `Vibrate` button, which when clicked, causes the phone to shake. The button's `onclick` event handler function is called `vibrateDevice` and is seen in the following example. This function calls the `makeCall` function and passes the `playSound` command with –1 passed as the additional parameter. This call causes the phone to vibrate. It uses the `playSound` command because the iPhone treats vibrations and short system sounds as sounds.

```
function vibrateDevice(event)
{
    //the -1 indicator causes the phone to vibrate
    makeCall("playSound", -1);
}
```

Because vibration and system sounds are treated the same playing a system sound is almost identical to vibrating the phone. The Sound button's `onclick` event handler is called `playSound`. As you can see in the following code, the only difference between it and `vibrateDevice` is the second parameter.

If a 0 is passed as the second parameter, the laser.wav file included in the DeviceCatalog project's resources is played as a system sound. System sound audio files must be less than five seconds long or they cannot be played as sounds. Audio files longer than this are played using the `play` command, which is covered later in this section.

```
function playSound(event)
{
    //the 0 indicator causes the phone to play the laser sound
    makeCall("playSound", 0);
}
```

The `makeCall` function used in the previous code exists completely in JavaScript and can be seen in the following code. The `makeCall` function consists of two portions. The first queues up the message if it cannot be sent immediately. The second sends the message to underlying Objective-C code for handling. The method used to pass the message is to change the `window.location` property to a nonexistent URL, `call`, with both parameters passed to the function as parameters of the URL.

```
function makeCall(command, dataString){
    var messageString = "cmd="+command+"&msg="+dataString;
    if(storeMessage || !canSend){
        messages.push(messageString);
    }
    else{
        storeMessage = true;
        window.location = "call?"+messageString;
    }
}
```

Setting the URL in this way causes a message, including the URL and its parameters, to be sent to an Objective-C component that is part of the underlying QuickConnectiPhone framework. This Objective-C component is designed to terminate the loading of the new page and pass the command and the message it was sent to the framework's command-handling code. To see how this is done, see Section 2.

The `playSound` and the `logMessage`, `rec`, and `play` commands are unidirectional, which means that communication from JavaScript to Objective-C with no data expected back occurs. The remaining unidirectional standard commands all cause data to be sent from the Objective-C components back to JavaScript.

The passing of data back to JavaScript is handled in two ways. An example of the first is used to transfer acceleration information in the x, y, and z coordinates by a call to the `handleRequest` JavaScript function, described in Chapter 2, "JavaScript Modularity and iPhone Applications." The call uses the `accel` command and the x, y, and z coordinates being passed as a JavaScript object from the Objective-C components of the framework.

The mappings.js file indicates that the `accel` command is mapped to the `displayAccelerationVCF` function, as shown in the following line.

```
mapCommandToVCF('accel', displayAccelerationVCF);
```

This causes `displayAccelerationVCF` to be called each time the accelerometers detect motion. This function is responsible for handling all acceleration events. In the DeviceCatalog example application, the function simply inserts the x, y, and z acceleration values into an HTML div. You should change this function to use these values for your application.

The second way to send data back to JavaScript uses a call to the `handleJSONRequest` JavaScript function. It works much like the `handleRequest` function described in Chapter 2, but expects a JSON string as its second parameter. This function is a façade for the `handleRequest` function. As shown in the following code, it simply converts the JSON string that is its second parameter into a JavaScript object and passes the command and the new object to the `handleRequest` method. This method of data transfer is used to reply to a GPS location request initiated by a `makeCall("loc")` call and the request to show a date and time picker.

```
function handleJSONRequest(cmd, parametersString){
    var paramsArray = null;
    if(parametersString){
        var paramsArray = JSON.parse(parametersString);
    }
    handleRequest(cmd, paramsArray);
}
```

In both cases, the resulting data is converted to a JSON string and then passed to `handleJSONRequest`. For more information on JSON, see Appendix A, "Introduction to JSON."

Because JSON libraries are available in both JavaScript and Objective-C, JSON becomes a good way to pass complex information between the two languages in an application. A simple example of this is the onclick handlers for the starting and stopping of recording and playing back audio files.

The `playRecording` handler is typical of all handlers for the user interface buttons that activate device behaviors. As shown in the following example, it creates a JavaScript array, adds two values, converts the array to a JSON string, and then executes the `makeCall` function with the `play` command.

```
function playRecording(event)
{
    var params = new Array();
    params[0] = "recordedFile.caf";
    params[1] = "start";
    makeCall("play", JSON.stringify(params));
}
```

To stop playing a recording, a `makeCall` is also issued with the `play` command, as shown in the previous example, but instead of the second param being `start`, it is set to `stop`. The `terminatePlaying` function in the main.js file implements this behavior.

Starting and stopping the recording of an audio file is done in the same way as `playRecording` and `terminatePlaying` except that instead of the `play` command, `rec` is used. Making the implementation of the starting and stopping of these related capabilities similar makes it much easier for you to add these behaviors to your application.

As seen earlier in this section, some device behaviors, such as vibrate require communication only from the JavaScript to the Objective-C handlers. Others, such as retrieving the current GPS coordinates or the results of a picker, require communication in both directions. Figure 4.1 shows the DeviceCatalog application with GPS information.

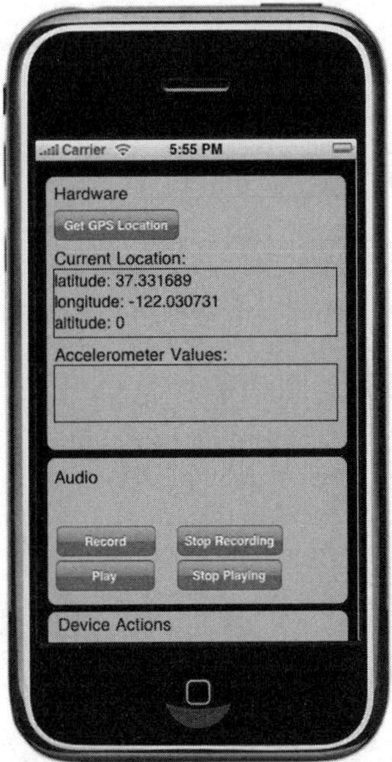

Figure 4.1 The DeviceCatalog example application showing GPS information.

As with some of the unidirectional examples already examined, communication starts in the JavaScript of your application. The `getGPSLocation` function in the main.js file initiates the communication using the `makeCall` function. Notice that as in the earlier examples, `makeCall` returns nothing. `makeCall` uses an asynchronous communication protocol to communicate with the Objective-C side of the library even when the communication is bidirectional, so no return value is available.

```
function getGPSLocation(event)
{
    document.getElementById('locDisplay').innerText = '';
    makeCall("loc");
}
```

Because the communication is asynchronous, as AJAX is, a callback function needs to be created and called to receive the GPS informartion. In the QuickConnectiPhone framework, this is accomplished by creating a mapping in the mapping file that maps the command `showLoc` to a function:

```
mapCommandToVCF('showLoc', displayLocationVCF);
```

In this case, it is mapped to the `displayLocationVCF` view control function. This simple example function is used only to display the current GPS location in a div on the screen. Obviously, these values can also be used to compute distances to be stored in a database or to be sent to a server using the ServerAccessObject described in Chapter 8, "Remote Data Access."

```
function displayLocationVCF(data, paramArray){
    document.getElementById('locDisplay').innerText = 'latitude:
'+paramArray[0]+'\nlongitude: '+paramArray[1]+'\naltitude:
'+paramArray[2];
}
```

Displaying a picker, such as the standard date and time picker, and then displaying the selected results is similar to the previous example. This process also begins with a call from JavaScript to the device-handling code. In this case, the event handler function of the button is the `showDateSelector` function found in the main.js file.

```
function showDateSelector(event)
{
    makeCall("showDate", "DateTime");
}
```

As with the GPS example, a mapping is also needed. This mapping maps the `showPickResults` command to the `displayPickerSelectionVCF` view control function, as shown in the following:

```
mapCommandToVCF('showPickResults', displayPickerSelectionVCF);
```

The function to which the command is mapped inserts the results of the user's selection in a simple div, as shown in the following code. Obviously, this information can be used in many ways.

```
function displayPickerSelectionVCF(data, paramArray){
    document.getElementById('pickerResults').innerHTML = paramArray[0];
```

Some uses of `makeCall`, such as the earlier examples in this section, communicate unidirectionally from the JavaScript to the Objective-C device handlers. Those just examined use bidirectional communication to and from handlers. Another type of communication that is possible with the device is unidirectionally from the device to your JavaScript code. An example of this is accelerometer information use.

The Objective-C handler for acceleration events, see Section 2 to see the code, makes a JavaScript `handleRequest` call directly passing the `accel` command. The following `accel` command is mapped to the `displayAccelerationVCF` view control function.

```
mapCommandToVCF('accel', displayAccelerationVCF);
```

As with the other VCFs, this one inserts the acceleration values into a div.

```
function displayAccelerationVCF(data, param){
    document.getElementById('accelDisplay').innerText ='x:
'+param.x+'\ny: '+param.y+'\nz: '+param.z;
}
```

One difference between this function and the others is that instead of an array being passed, this function has an object passed as its `param` parameter. Section 2 shows how this object was created from information passed from the Objective-C acceleration event handler.

This section has shown you how to add some of the most commonly requested iPhone behaviors to your JavaScript-based application. Section 2 shows the Objective-C portions of the framework that support this capability.

Section 2: Objective-C Device Activation

This section assumes you are familiar with Objective-C and how it is used to create iPhone applications. If you are not familiar with this, Erica Sadun's book *The iPhone Developer's Cookbook* is available from Pearson Publishing. If you just want to use the QuickConnectiPhone framework to write JavaScript applications for the iPhone, you do not have to read this section.

Using Objective-C to vibrate the iPhone is one of the easiest behaviors to implement. It can be done with the following single line of code if you include the AudioToolbox framework in the resources of your project.

```
AudioServicesPlaySystemSound(kSystemSoundID_Vibrate);
```

The question then becomes, "How can I get the `AudioServicesPlaySystemSound` function to be called when the UIWebView is told to change its location?"

The QuickConnectViewController implements the `shouldStartLoadWithRequest` delegate method. Because the delegate of the embedded UIWebView, called `aWebView`, is set to be the QuickConnectViewController this method is called every time the embedded UIWebView is told to change its location. The following code and line 90 of the QuickConnectViewController.m file show this delegate being set.

```
[aWebView setDelegate:self];
```

The basic behavior of the `shouldStartLoadWithRequest` function is straightforward. It is designed to enable you to write code that decides if the new page requested should actually be loaded. The QuickConnectiPhone framework takes advantage of the decision-making capability to disallow page loading by any of the requests made by the JavaScript calls shown in Section 1 and execute other Objective-C code.

The `shouldStartLoadWithRequest` method has several parameters that are available for use. These include

- `curWebView`—The UIWebView containing your JavaScript application.
- `request`—A NSURLRequest containing the new URL among other items.
- `navigationType`—A UIWebViewNavigationType that can be used to determine if the request is the result of the user selecting a link or if it was generated as a result of some other action.

```
-(BOOL)webView:(UIWebView *)curWebView
   shouldStartLoadWithRequest:(NSURLRequest *)request
navigationType:(UIWebViewNavigationType)navigationType
```

The URL assembled by the `makeCall` JavaScript function that causes the device to vibrate, `call?cmd=playSound&msg=-1` is contained in the `request` object and is easily retrieved as a string by passing the `URL` message to it. This message returns an NSURL-type object, which is then passed the `absoluteString` message. Thus, an NSString pointer representing the URL is obtained. This string, seen as `url` in the following code, can then be split into an array using the ? as the splitting delimiter, yielding an array of NSString pointers.

```
NSString *url = [[request URL] absoluteString];
NSArray *urlArray = [url componentsSeparatedByString:@"?"];
```

`urlArray` contains two elements. The first is the `call` portion of the URL and the second is the command string `cmd=playSound&msg=-1`. To determine which command to act on and any parameters that might need to be used, in this case the –1, the command string requires further parsing. This is done by splitting the `commandString` at the & character. This creates another array called `urlParamsArray`.

```
NSString *commandString = [urlArray objectAtIndex:1];
NSArray *urlParamsArray = [commandString
componentsSeparatedByString:@"&"];
//the command is the first parameter in the URL
cmd = [[[urlParamsArray objectAtIndex:0]
componentsSeparatedByString:@"="] objectAtIndex:1];
```

In this case, requesting that the device to vibrate, the first element of the `urlParamsArray` array becomes `cmd=playSound` and the second is `msg=-1`. Thus, splitting the elements of the urlParamsArray can retrieve the command to be executed and the parameter. The = character is the delimiter to split each element of the `urlParamsArray`.

Lines 1– 3 in the following example retrieve the parameter sent as the value associated with the `msg` key in the URL as the NSString `parameterArrayString`. Because the JavaScript that assembled the URL converts all items that are this value to JSON, this NSString is an object that has been converted into JSON format. This includes numbers, such as the current example, and strings, arrays, or other parameters passed from the JavaScript. Additionally, if spaces or other special characters appear in the data, the UIWebView escapes them as part of the URL. Therefore, lines 6–8 in the following code is needed to unescape any special characters in the JSON string.

```
1 NSString *parameterArrayString = [[[urlParamsArray
2   objectAtIndex:1] componentsSeparatedByString:@"="]
3   objectAtIndex:1];
4   //remove any encoding added as the UIWebView has
5   //escaped the URL characters.
6   parameterArrayString = [parameterArrayString
7     stringByReplacingPercentEscapesUsingEncoding:
8     NSASCIIStringEncoding];
9   SBJSON *generator = [SBJSON alloc];
10   NSError *error;
11   paramsToPass = [[NSMutableArray alloc]
12   initWithArray:[generator
13      objectWithString:parameterArrayString
14      error:&error]];
15   if([paramsToPass count] == 0){
16        //if there was no array of data sent then it must have
17     //been a string that was sent as the only parameter.
18     [paramsToPass addObject:parameterArrayString];
19   }
20   [generator release];
```

Lines 9–14 in the previous code contain the code to convert the JSON string `parameterArrayString` to a native Objective-C NSArray. Line 9 allocates a SBJSON generator object. The generator object is then sent the `objectWithString` message seen in the following:

```
- (id)objectWithString:(NSString*)jsonrep error:(NSError**)error;
```

This multipart message is passed a JSON string, in this case `parameterArrayString`, and an NSError pointer `error`. The `error` pointer is assigned if an error occurs during the conversion process. If no error happens, it is nil.

The return value of this message is in this case the number –1. If a JavaScript array is stringified, it is an NSArray pointer, or if it is a JavaScript string, it is an NSString pointer. If a JavaScript custom object type is passed, the returned object is an NSDictionary pointer.

At this point, having retrieved the command and any parameters needed to act on the command, it is possible to use an `if` or `case` statement to do the actual computation.

Such a set of conditionals is, however, not optimal because they have to be modified each time a command is added or removed. In Chapter 2, this same problem is solved in the JavaScript portion of the QuickConnectiPhone architecture by implementing a front controller function called `handleRequest` that contains calls to implementations of application controllers. Because the problem is the same here, an Objective-C version of `handleRequest` should solve the current problem. Section 3 covers the implementation of the front controllers and application controllers in Objective-C. The following line of code retrieves an instance of the QuickConnect object and passes it the `handleRequest withParameters` multimessage. No further computation is required within the `shouldStartLoadWithRequest` delegate method.

```
[[QuickConnect getInstance] handleRequest:cmd withParameters:paramsToPass];
```

Because the QuickConnect objects' `handleRequest` message is used, there must be a way of mapping the command to the required functionality as shown in Chapter 2 using JavaScript. The `QCCommandMappings` object found in the QCCommandMappings.m and .h files of the QCObjC group contains all the mappings for Business Control Objects (BCO) and View Control Objects (VCO) for this example.

The following code is the `mapCommands` method of the `QCCommandMappings` object that is called when the application starts. It is passed an implementation of an application controller that is used to create the mappings of command to functionality. An explanation of the code for the `mapCommandToVCO` message and the call of `mapCommands` are found in Section 3.

```
1 + (void) mapCommands:(QCAppController*)aController{
2    [aController mapCommandToVCO:@"logMessage" withFunction:@"LoggingVCO"];
3    [aController mapCommandToVCO:@"playSound" withFunction:@"PlaySoundVCO"];
4    [aController mapCommandToBCO:@"loc" withFunction:@"LocationBCO"];
5    [aController mapCommandToVCO:@"sendloc" withFunction:@"LocationVCO"];
6    [aController mapCommandToVCO:@"showDate" withFunction:@"DatePickerVCO"];
7    [aController mapCommandToVCO:@"sendPickResults"
withFunction:@"PickResultsVCO"];
8    [aController mapCommandToVCO:@"play" withFunction:@"PlayAudioVCO"];
9    [aController mapCommandToVCO:@"rec" withFunction:@"RecordAudioVCO"];
10 }
```

Line 3 of the previous code is pertinent to the current example of vibrating the device. As seen earlier in this section, the command received from the JavaScript portion of the application is `playSound`. By sending this command as the first parameter of the `mapCommandToVCO` message and `PlaySoundVCO` as the parameter for the second portion, `withFunction`, a link is made that causes the application controller to send a `doCommand` message with the –1 parameter to the `PlaySoundVCO` class. As you can see, all the other commands in the DeviceCatalog example that are sent from JavaScript are mapped here.

The code for the `PlaySoundVCO` to which the `playSound` command is mapped is found in the PlaySoundVCO.m and PlaySoundVCO.h files. The `doCommand` method contains all the object's behavior.

To play a system sound, a predefined sound, of which vibrate is the only one at the time of writing this book, must be used or a system sound must be generated from a sound file. The `doCommand` of the `PlaySoundVCO` class shows examples of both of these types of behavior.

```
1 + (id) doCommand:(NSArray*) parameters{
2     SystemSoundID aSound =
3       [((NSNumber*)[parameters objectAtIndex:1]) intValue];
4     if(aSound == -1){
5         aSound = kSystemSoundID_Vibrate;
6     }
7     else{
8         NSString *soundFile =
9          [[NSBundle mainBundle] pathForResource:@"laser"
10                 ofType:@"wav"];
11         NSURL *url = [NSURL fileURLWithPath:soundFile];
12         //if the audio file is takes to long to play
13         //you will get a -1500 error
14         OSStatus error = AudioServicesCreateSystemSoundID(
15           (CFURLRef) url, &aSound );
16     }
17     AudioServicesPlaySystemSound(aSound);
18     return nil;
19 }
```

As seen in line 4 in the previous example, if the parameter with the index of 1 has a value of –1, the `SystemSoundID aSound` variable is set to the defined `kSystemSoundID_Vibrate` value. If it is not, a system sound is created from the laser.wav file found in the resources group of the application, and the `aSound` variable is set to an identifier generated for the new system sound.

In either case, the C function `AudioServicesPlaySystemSound` is called and the sound is played or the device vibrates. If the device is an iPod Touch, requests for vibration are ignored by the device. In an actual application that has multiple sounds, this function can easily be expanded by passing other numbers as indicators of which sound should be played.

Because the `SystemSoundID` type variable is actually numeric, the system sounds should be generated at application start and the SystemSoundIDs for each of them should be passed to the JavaScript portion of the application for later use. This avoids the computational load of recreating the system sound each time a sound is required, and therefore, increases the quality of the user's experience because there is no delay of the playing of the sound.

Having now seen the process of passing commands from JavaScript to Objective-C and how to vibrate the device or play a short sound, it is now easy to see and understand how to pass a command to Objective-C and have the results returned to the JavaScript portion of the application.

Because these types of communication behave similarly, GPS location detection, which is a popular item in iPhone applications, is shown as an example. It uses this bidirectional, JavaScript-Objective-C communication capability of the QuickConnectiPhone framework.

As with the handling of all the commands sent from the JavaScript framework, there must be a mapping of the `loc` command so that the data can be retrieved and a response sent back.

```
[aController mapCommandToBCO:@"loc" withFunction:@"LocationBCO"];
[aController mapCommandToVCO:@"sendloc" withFunction:@"LocationVCO"];
```

In this case, there are two mappings: The first is to a BCO and the second is to a VCO. As discussed in Chapter 2, BCOs do data retrieval and VCOs are used for data presentation.

Because BCOs for a given command are executed prior to all of the VCOs by the QuickConnectiPhone framework, a `doCommand` message is first sent to the `LocationBCO` class, which retrieves and returns the GPS data. The following `doCommand` method belongs to the `LocationBCO` class. It makes the calls required to get the device to begin finding its GPS location.

```
+ (id) doCommand:(NSArray*) parameters{
    QuickConnectViewController *controller = (QuickConnectViewController*)[parame-
ters objectAtIndex:0];
    [[controller locationManager] startUpdatingLocation];
    return nil;
}
```

This method starts the GPS location hardware by retrieving the first item in the parameter's array that is passed into the method and informing it to start the hardware. The framework always sets the first parameter to be the `QuickConnectViewController` so that it can be used if needed by BCOs or VCOs associated with any command. In all of the Objective-C BCOs and VCOs any parameters sent from JavaScript begin with an index of 1.

The `QuickConnectViewController` object has a built in `CLLocationManager` attribute called `locationManager` that is turned on and off as needed by your application. It is important not to leave this manager running any longer than needed because it uses large amounts of battery power. Therefore, the previous code turns the location hardware on by sending it a `startUpdatingLocation` message each time a location is needed. The location hardware is turned off once the location is found.

`CLLocationManager` objects behave in an asynchronous manner. This means that when a request is made for location information, a predefined callback function is called after the location has been determined. This predefined function allows you access to the location manager and two locations: a previously determined location and a current location.

The location manager works by gradually refining the device's location. As it does this, it calls `didUpdateToLocation` several times. The following code example finds out how long it takes to determine the new location. Line 9 determines if this is less than 5.0 seconds and if it is terminates the location search.

```
1  (void)locationManager:(CLLocationManager *)manager
2      didUpdateToLocation:(CLLocation *)newLocation
3        fromLocation:(CLLocation *)oldLocation
4 {
5     // If it's a relatively recent event, turn off updates to save power
6     NSDate* eventDate = newLocation.timestamp;
7     NSTimeInterval howRecent =
8             [eventDate timeIntervalSinceNow];
9     if (abs(howRecent) < 5.0){
10         [manager stopUpdatingLocation];
11         NSMutableArray *paramsToPass =
12           [[NSMutableArray alloc] initWithCapacity:2];
13         [paramsToPass addObject:self];
14         [paramsToPass addObject:newLocation];
15         [[QuickConnect getInstance]
16             handleRequest:@"sendloc"
17               withParameters:paramsToPass];
18     }
19     // else skip the event and process the next one.
20 }
```

Having terminated the location search, the code then sends a message to the QuickConnect front controller class stating that it should handle a `sendloc` request with the `QuickConnectViewController`, `self`, and the new location passed as an additional parameter.

The `sendloc` command is mapped to the `LocationVCO` handler whose `doCommand` method is seen in the following example. This method retrieves the UIWebView called `webView` from the `QuickConnectViewController` that made the original request for GPS location information. It then places the GPS information into the NSArray called `passingArray`.

To pass the GPS information back to the `webView` object, the NSArray within which it is contained must be converted into a JSON string. The same SBJSON class used earlier to create an array from a JSON string is now used to create a NSString from the NSArray. This is done on lines 21 and 22:

```
1 + (id) doCommand:(NSArray*) parameters{
2     QuickConnectViewController *controller =
3     (QuickConnectViewController*)[parameters
4       objectAtIndex:0];
5     UIWebView *webView = [controller webView];
6     CLLocation *location = (CLLocation*)[parameters
7       objectAtIndex:1];
```

```

    NSMutableArray *passingArray = [[NSMutableArray alloc]
      initWithCapacity:3];
     [passingArray addObject: [NSNumber numberWithDouble:
     location.coordinate.latitude]];
     [passingArray addObject: [NSNumber numberWithDouble:
      location.coordinate.longitude]];
     [passingArray addObject: [NSNumber numberWithFloat:
     location.altitude]];

     SBJSON *generator = [SBJSON alloc];

     NSError *error;
     NSString *paramsToPass = [generator
      stringWithObject:passingArray error:&error];
     [generator release];
     NSString *jsString = [[NSString alloc]
     initWithFormat:@"handleJSONRequest('showLoc', '%@')",
       paramsToPass];
   [webView
     stringByEvaluatingJavaScriptFromString:jsString];
     return nil;
}
```

After converting the GPS location information into a JSON string representing an array of numbers, a call is made to the JavaScript engine inside the `webView` object. This is done by first creating an NSString that is the JavaScript to be executed. In this example, it is a `handleJSONRequest` that is passed `showLoc` as the command and the JSON GPS information as a string. As seen in Section 1, this request causes the GPS data to appear in a div in the HTML page being displayed.

Having seen this example, you can now look at the `DatePickerVCO` and `PickResultsVCO` in the DeviceCatalog example and see how this same approach is used to display the standard date and time selectors, called pickers, that are available in Objective-C. Although predefined pickers available using JavaScript within the UIWebView, they are not as nice from the user's point of view as the standard ones available from within Objective-C. By using these standard ones and any custom ones you may choose to define, your hybrid application will have a smoother user experience.

Section 3: Objective-C Implementation of the QuickConnectiPhone Architecture

The code shown in Sections 1 and 2 depends heavily on an implementation in Objective-C of the same architecture, which is explained in Chapter 2. This section shows how to implement the architecture in Objective-C. To see a full explanation of each component, see Chapter 2, which contains the JavaScript implementation.

As in the JavaScript implementation, all requests for application behavior are handled via a front controller. The front controller is implemented as the class `QuickConnect`, the source for which is found in the QuickConnect.m and QuickConnect.h files. Because messages sent to `QuickConnect` might need to be made from many different locations throughout an application, this class is a singleton.

Singleton classes are written so that only one instantiated object of that class can be allocated within an application. If done correctly, there is always a way to obtain a pointer to this single object from anywhere in the application. With the `QuickConnect` singleton object, this is accomplished by implementing a class method `getInstance` that returns the single `QuickConnect` instance that is allocated the first time this method is called.

Because it is a class method, a `getInstance` message can be sent to the class without instantiating a `QuickConnect` object. When called, it returns a pointer to the underlying `QuickConnect` instance. As seen in the following code, this is accomplished by assigning an instance of the class to a statically defined `QuickConnect` pointer.

```
+ (QuickConnect*)getInstance{
    //since this line is declared static
    //it will only be executed once.
    static QuickConnect *mySelfQC = nil;

    @synchronized([QuickConnect class]) {
        if (mySelfQC == nil) {
            mySelfQC = [QuickConnect singleton];
            [mySelfQC init];
        }
    }
    return mySelfQC;
}
```

The singleton message sent prior to init uses the behavior defined in the `QuickConnect` objects' superclass `FTSWAbstractSingleton`. This superclass allocates the embedded singleton behavior such as overriding new, clone, and other methods that someone might incorrectly attempt to use to allocate another `QuickConnect` instance. Because of this, only the `getInstance` method can be used to create and use a `QuickConnect` object. As with all well-formed objects in Objective-C, after a `QuickConnect` object has been allocated, it must be initialized.

Both the allocation and initialization of the object happen only if no `QuickConnect` object has been assigned to the `mySelfQC` attribute. Additionally, because of the synchronization call surrounding the check for the instantiated `QuickConnect` object, the checking and initialization are thread safe.

`- (void) handleRequest: (NSString*) aCmd withParameters:(NSArray*) parameters` is another method of the `QuickConnect` class. Just as with the JavaScript `handleRequest(aCmd, parameters)` function from Chapter 2, this method is the way to request functionality be executed in your application.

A command string and an array of parameters are passed to the method. In the following example, lines 3–9 show that a series of messages are sent to the application controller. Lines 3 and 4 first execute any VCOs associated with the command. If the command and parameters pass validation, any BCOs associated with the command are executed by a `dispatchToBCO` message. This message returns an `NSMutableArray` that contains the original `parameters` array data to which has been added any data accumulated by any BCO object that might have been called.

```
1 - (void) handleRequest: (NSString*) aCmd
2         withParameters:(NSArray*) parameters{
3   if([self->theAppController dispatchToValCO:aCmd
4      withParameters:parameters] != nil){
5     NSMutableArray *newParameters =
6       [self->theAppController dispatchToBCO:aCmd
7               withParameters:parameters];
8        [self->theAppController dispatchToVCO:aCmd
9               withParameters:newParameters];
10   }
11 }
```

After the completion of the call to `dispatchToBCO:withParameters`, a `dispatchToVCO:withParameters` message is sent. This causes any VCOs also associated with the given command to be executed.

By using the `handleRequest:withParameters` method for all requests for functionality, each request goes through a three-step process.

1. Validation.
2. Execution of business rules (BCO).
3. Execution of view changes (VCO).

As in the JavaScript implementation, each `dispatchTo` method is a façade. In this case, the underlying Objective-C method is `dispatchToCO:withParameters`.

This method first retrieves all the command objects associated with the `default` command in `aMap` the passed parameter. `aMap` contains either BCOs, VCOs, or ValCOs depending on which façade method was called. These default command objects, if any, are retrieved and used for all commands. If you want to have certain command objects used for all commands, you do not need to map them to each individual command. Map them to the `default` command once instead.

For the retrieved command objects to be used, they must be sent a message. The message to be sent is `doCommand`. Lines 19–23 in the following example show this message being retrieved as a selector and the `performSelector` message being passed. This causes the `doCommand` message you have implemented in your `QCCommandObject` to be executed.

```
1 - (id) dispatchToCO: (NSString*)command withParameters:
2          (NSArray*)parameters andMap:(NSDictionary*)aMap{
3     //create a mutable array that contains all of
```

```
    // the existing parameters.
    NSMutableArray *resultArray;
    if(parameters == nil){
       resultArray = [[NSMutableArray alloc]
                          initWithCapacity:0];
   }
    else{
       resultArray = [NSMutableArray
                          arrayWithArray:parameters];
    }
    //set the result to be something so
    //that if no mappings are made the
    //execution will continue.
    id result = @"Continue";
    if([aMap objectForKey:@"default"] != nil){
       SEL aSelector = @selector(doCommand);
       while((result = [((QCCommandObject*)
           [aMap objectForKey:@"default"])
           performSelector:aSelector
               withObject:parameters]) != nil){
           if(aMap == self->businessMap){
             [resultArray addObject:result];
           }
       }
     }
     //if all of the default command objects' method calls
     //return something, execute all of the custom ones.
     if(result != nil && [aMap objectForKey:command] !=
          nil){
        NSArray *theCommandObjects =
            [aMap objectForKey:command];
        int numCommandObjects = [theCommandObjects count];
        for(int i = 0; i < numCommandObjects; i++){
           QCCommandObject *theCommand =
              [theCommandObjects objectAtIndex:i];
           result = [theCommand doCommand:parameters];
           if(result == nil){
               resultArray = nil;
               break;
           }
           if(aMap == self->businessMap){
              [resultArray addObject:result];
           }
       }
   }
   if(aMap == self->businessMap){
```

```
        return resultArray;
    }
    return result;
}
```

After all the `doCommand` messages are sent to any `QCCommandObjects` you mapped to the `default` command, the same is done for `QCCommandObjects` you mapped to the command passed into the method as a parameter. These `QCCommandObjects` have the same reasons for existence as the control functions in the JavaScript implementation. Because `QCCommandObjects` contain all the behavior code for your application, an example is of one is helpful in understanding how they are created.

`QCCommandObject` is the parent class of `LoggingVCO`. As such, `LoggingVCO` must implement the `doCommand` method. The entire contents of the LoggingVCO.m file found in the DeviceCatalog example follows. Its `doCommand` method writes to the log file of the

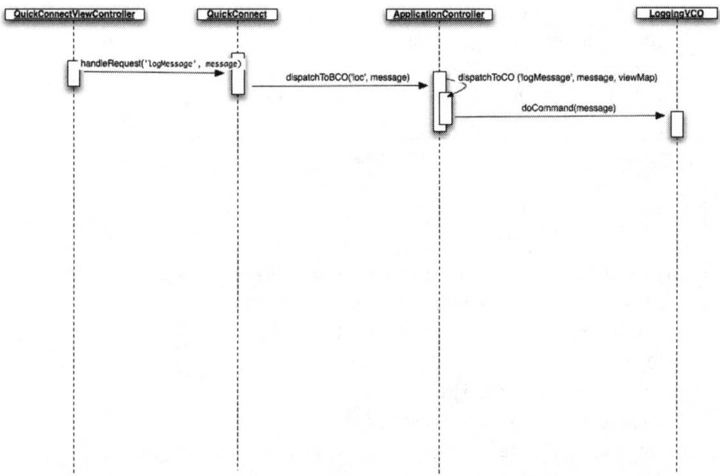

Figure 4.2 A sequence diagram shows the methods called in Objective-C to handle a request to log a JavaScript debug message.

running application. This VCO logs debug messages generated from within the JavaScript code of your application. Figure 4.2 shows the calls required to accomplish this.

The `doCommand` method of the `LoggingVCO` class is small. All `doCommand` methods for the different types of command objects should always be small. They should do one thing only and do it well. If you find that a `doCommand` method you are working on is getting large, you might want to consider splitting it into logical components and creating more than one command object class. The reason for this is that if these methods become long, they are probably doing more than one thing.

In the following example, the "one thing" the `LoggingVCO` does is log messages to the debug console in Xcode. Obviously, this small component can be reused with many commands in combination with other command objects.

The behavior of this VCO consists of a single line that executes the `NSLog` function. In doing so, the first object in the parameters array is appended to a static string and written out.

```
#import "LoggingVCO.h"



@implementation LoggingVCO

+ (id) doCommand:(NSArray*) parameters{
    NSLog(@"JavaScriptMessage: %@",
            [parameters objectAtIndex:1]);
    return nil;
}

@end
```

For this logging to occur, a mapping must be generated between the `logMessage` command and the `LoggingVCO` class. As in the JavaScript implementation, this is done by adding `logMessage` as a key and the name of the `LoggingVCO` class as a value to a map.

Mapping is done in the QCCommandMappings.m file. The code that follows comes from this file in the DeviceCatalog example and maps `logMessage` to the `LoggingVCO` class.

```
[aController mapCommandToVCO:@"logMessage"
    withFunction:@"LoggingVCO"];
```

The application controller is passed the `mapCommandToVCO:withFunction` message where the command is the first parameter and the VCO name is the second. This method and others like it used to map the other command object types are façades. Each of these façade methods calls the underlying `mapCommandToCO` method.

This `mapCommandToCO` method enables multiple command objects to be mapped to a single command by mapping the command to an `NSMutableArray`. This array is then used to contain the `Class` objects that match the class name passed in as the second parameter. The following code shows the implementation of the `mapCommandToCO method`.

```
- (void) mapCommandToCO:(NSString*)aCommand
          withFunction:(NSString*)aClassName
          toMap:(NSMutableDictionary*)aMap{
    NSMutableArray *controlObjects =
          [[aMap objectForKey:aCommand] retain];
    if(controlObjects == nil){
        NSMutableArray *tmpCntrlObjs =
            [[NSMutableArray alloc] initWithCapacity:1];
        [aMap setObject: tmpCntrlObjs forKey:aCommand];
```

```
            controlObjects = tmpCntrlObjs;
            [tmpCntrlObjs release];
        }
        //Get the control object's class
        //for the given name and add an object
        //of that type to the array for the command.
        Class aClass = NSClassFromString(aClassName);
        if(aClass != nil){
           [controlObjects addObject:aClass];
        }
        else{
            MESSAGE( unable to find the %@ class.
              Make sure that it exists under this
              name and try again.");
        }
}
```

The addition of the Class objects to an `NSMutableArray` enables any number of command objects of similar type, VCOs, BCOs, or others to be mapped to the same command and then executed individually in the order that the `mapCommandTo` messages were sent. Thus, you can have several VCOs execute sequentially.

For example, you can use a VCO that displays a UIView followed by another that changes another UIView's opacity, and then follow that up by logging a message. Sending three `mapCommandToVCO` messages with the same command but three different command object names would do this.

Several other examples of BCOs and VCOs exist in the DeviceCatalog example. Each one is activated as requests are made from the JavaScript portion of the application.

Summary

This chapter showed you how to activate several desirable features of iPhone or iPod Touch devices from within your JavaScript application. Using features such as GPS location, the accelerometer values, vibrating the phone, and playing sounds and audio increase the richness of your application.

By looking at the examples included in the DeviceCatalog and if you work in Objective-C, you should be able to add additional features such as scanning the Bonjour network for nearby devices, adding, removing, and retrieving contacts from the contacts application, or adding, removing, and retrieving other built in behaviors that are available in Objective-C applications.

Your JavaScript application can, using the approach described in this chapter, do most anything a pure Objective-C application can do. An example of this is in Chapter 8, where you learn how to embed Google maps into any application without losing the look and feel of Apple's Map application.

5

Hybrid Applications, GPS, Acceleration, and Other Native Functions with PhoneGap

The PhoneGap library provides an alternative to using the QuickConnect framework discussed in Chapter 4, "GPS, Acceleration, and Other Native Functions with QuickConnect." Although it does not have the full range of features found in QuickConnect, it is, along with QuickConnect, a popular choice for accessing device information and behavior. The first section of this chapter explains how to access these native iPhone functionalities using the PhoneGap JavaScript API. The second section shows the JavaScript and Objective-C code that underlies the PhoneGap JavaScript API.

Section 1: JavaScript Device Activation

Because PhoneGap is undergoing development at the time of this writing, it has a limited number of native behaviors that are available. This section covers only those behaviors that have support on both the JavaScript and Objective-C sides of the application. There are placeholders in the code for behavior code not yet complete or functioning in PhoneGap at this time. These behaviors are not covered.

Table 5.1 lists the methods, functions, and attributes that are part of the working API. Unlike QuickConnectiPhone, these do not belong to a larger framework. As such, you are responsible for calling them directly. Because there is little safety checking in the active code, be sure that parameters passed to these functions are valid and not null.

As discussed in Chapter 4, QuickConnectiPhone includes the HTML, CSS, and JavaScript in the installed application on the device. PhoneGap does not. Instead, at startup, a generic Objective-C application, renamed as your application, temporarily loads these files from a web server to which they had previously been published (see Figure 5.1). To run the application, your device must have network connectivity. Therefore, do not expect your application to run correctly when the user is on an airplane or where connectivity is not available.

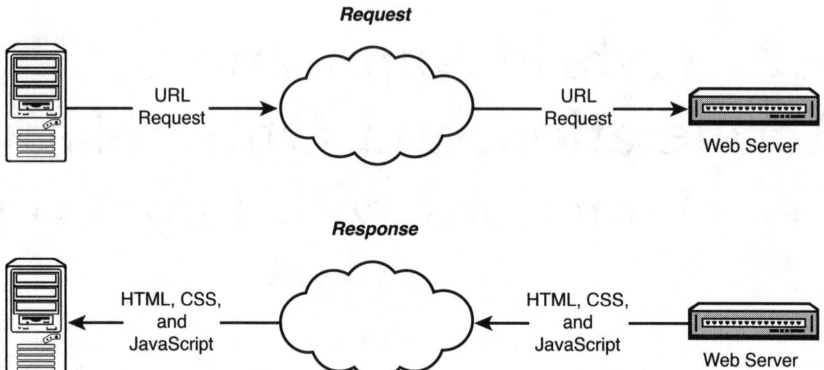

Figure 5.1 The startup request and response for PhoneGap applications used to obtain the HTML, CSS, and JavaScript that define the application

When a PhoneGap application starts loading its web components from the server, a call is made from the generic Objective-C application to JavaScript. This call sets a series of global variables that describe the device the application runs on. The `Device.init` method of the JavaScript API, usually called in a function that is assigned to be the `onload` event listener, exists to gather up the global variables set by the Objective-C portion of the application and stores them in attributes of PhoneGap's Device object. The Objective-C code that sets these device variables is discussed in Section 2.

```
init: function(model, version) {
.
.
.
      Device.available = __gap;
      Device.model = __gap_device_model;
      Device.version = __gap_device_version;
      Device.gapVersion = __gap_version;
      Device.uuid = __gap_device_uniqueid;
.
.
.
 }
```

The previous example shows code relevant to the iPhone and iPod Touch devices. Each of the global value names begins with __ (double underscore) and has a unique value. The `__gap` variable is used as a flag to indicate whether or not the JavaScript is run from within a PhoneGap application. This is required because at the time of this book's writing, the application's HTML, CSS, and JavaScript files are not included in any compiled, installed PhoneGap application but downloaded by the wrapper from the Internet. If your application's HTML, CSS, and JavaScript files are accessed by a web browser instead of a PhoneGap application, the `__gap` variable would be null and can be used as a flag later in your code.

The `__gap_device_model` variable contains a string that describes the device your application is running on, such as iPhone, iPod Touch, or iPhone Simulator. This variable also includes the device's OS version, which is in the `__gap_device_version` global variable. The device's globally unique id is in the `__gap_device_uniqueid` variable, and the version of PhoneGap is found in `__gap_version`. Each of these values is available for use either from the public device attributes seen in the snippet or from the global variables anywhere in your code. Table 5.1 describes each of the JavaScript functions that allow you to access device behaviors.

Table 5.1 **PhoneGap JavaScript API**

Element	Parameters	Behavior
`gotAcceleration()`	x—The acceleration value along the x-axis. y—The acceleration value along the y-axis. z—The acceleration value along the z-axis.	This function is not predefined. To receive accelerometer information, create this function somewhere in your application. When created, the Objective-C library can then call it and pass it the parameter values.
`Device.init()`	None	Gathers up the device information from global variables that were set when the application started. This information is placed in the Device object and includes: Device type (iPhone/iPodTouch) Device OS version Device UniqueID PhoneGap version
`Device.vibrate()`	None	Causes the phone to vibrate for the standard amount of time.

Table 5.1 **PhoneGap JavaScript API**

Element	Parameters	Behavior
`Device.sound()`	clip—A string that is the name and type of the sound file to be played. Example: "tweet.wav"	A sound file with this name must be in the Resources of your application or an execution error will happen.
`Device.Location.init()`	None	Causes location information already on the Objective-C side of the application to be sent to the JavaScript side for processing and/or display.
`Device.Location.callback`		This attribute of the Location object when set to a custom callback function causes a callback function to be executed when the GPS information is available.
`Device.Location.wait()`	func—A callback function is executed when the GPS information is available.	This is an alternative to the `Device.Location.init()` function.
`Device.exec()`	command—A command string that is passed to the Objective-C side of the application for processing. Examples: "vibrate," "sound," and "getLoc"	This is the function that handles all communication to the Objective-C side of the application. Each command sent triggers different native device behavior. This is the method you call from JavaScript if you created custom Objective-C code that you want executed.

The PGDeviceCatalog sample application includes a `Vibrate` button that when clicked causes the phone to shake. The button's `onclick` event handler function is called `vibrateDevice`. This function calls the `Device.vibrate` method that causes the device to vibrate.

```
function vibrateDevice(event)
{
      Device.vibrate();
}
```

The following `Device.vibrate` method is a façade for the Device object's `exec` method. It calls `Device.exec` and passes it the `vibrate` command. All the PhoneGap device behavior methods are actually façades of `Device.exec`, which is similar to `Device.vibrate`.

```
vibrate: function() {
      return Device.exec("vibrate")
}
```

The `Device.exec` function used in the previous code exists completely in JavaScript and is shown in the following code. Like QuickConnectiPhone, PhoneGap sets the URL and creates a message consisting of the URL and the command, such as `vibrate`, to be sent to an Objective-C component that is part of the underlying PhoneGap framework. This component is programmed to terminate the loading of a new page and evaluate which command has been sent. For more information on this process, see Section 2.

```
exec: function(command) {
      if (Device.available) {
            try {
                  document.location = "gap:" + command;
            } catch(e) {
                  console.log("Command '" + command +
                  "' has not been executed, because of exception: "
                  + e);
                  alert("Error executing command '" +
                  command + "'.")
            }
      }
}
```

In the catch portion of the previous code, there are two ways of notifying the user that something has gone wrong. The first, a `console.log` call, writes a message to Dashcode's console and works only when running in Dashcode, not on the device.

The second message uses an alert dialog. Because PhoneGap has implemented alert behavior in Objective-C, this is active on the device but according to Apple should never be used in iPhone applications. For more information on iPhone application user interface design, see Chapter 3, "Creating iPhone User Interfaces."

The `playSound` and `vibrate` methods are both unidirectional, which means there is communication from JavaScript to Objective-C with no data expected back. The `Device.Location.init` method is bidirectional and therefore expects to receive data from the Objective-C PhoneGap library. As shown in the following code, this init method is also a façade for the `Device.exec` method. In this case, the command passed is `getloc` as opposed to the `vibrate` command shown earlier.

Figure 5.2 shows a running PhoneGap application that has requested GPS location information. GPS information is also accessed by a façade that calls `Device.exec`.

```
init: function() {
.
.
```

```
.
        Device.exec("getloc");
.
.
.
}
```

In the PGDeviceCatalog example, the `Device.Location.init` method is called from within the `getGPS` listener function in the following code. It consists of four lines of code. The third line calls the `init` function and notifies the Objective-C library that its stored GPS data is needed.

```
function getGPS(event){
    Device.Location.callback = updateLocation;
    Device.Location.init();
}
```

The second line of `getGPS` informs the `Device.Location` object that the `updateLocation` function, also found in main.js, is to be called when the GPS data has been retrieved. In PhoneGap, this process is much faster than in QuickConnectiPhone

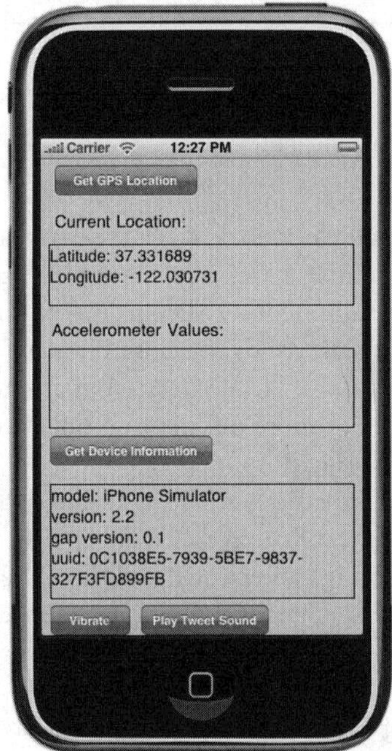

Figure 5.2 The PGDeviceCatalog example application showing the GPS and Device information

because the PhoneGap Objective-C library starts up the GPS hardware of the device as soon as the application is launched and shuts it down when the application exits.

By using the GPS hardware, the entire time the application runs all PhoneGap applications, even if they don't use the GPS data collected and stored, use large amounts of battery power. The GPS hardware uses so much battery power that Apple states that leaving it on for the run time of an application constitutes being a "poor iPhone neighbor." Using this strategy can easily drain the battery of the device leaving insufficient power for phone calls and the running of other applications. Because of this, PhoneGap applications should be designed in such a way that they are intended to run only for short periods of time even if they do not use GPS data. Because QuickConnectiPhone starts the GPS hardware when you request GPS information and shuts it down when the location is found, they can be designed to be run for much longer periods of time.

To receive the accelerometer data, a function called `gotAcceleration(x, y, z)` must be implemented somewhere in your application. In the PGDeviceCatalog example application, this is found in the main.js file, as shown in the following.

```
function gotAcceleration(x, y, z){
      document.getElementById('accelDisplay').innerHTML =
            'X: '+x+'<br/>Y: '+y+' <br/>Z: '+z;
}
```

This implementation of the `gotAcceleration` function displays only the accelerometer values. In your implementation, you might want to do some evaluation of the data such as a low pass filter or use it to cause some sort of change in the UI other than displaying the numerical data.

Because the simulator doesn't have accelerometer access to see this information displayed, you must run the application on an actual device. When you do, the `gotAcceleration` function is called each time one of the accelerometers detects a change.

It is also possible to play an audio file from within JavaScript using the PhoneGap library. An example of this is the `playTweetSound` function shown in the following code. It calls the `Device.playSound` method that is a `Device.exec` façade like the `Device.vibrate` method mentioned previously.

```
function playTweetSound(event)
{
    Device.playSound('bird.mp3');
}
```

The `playSound` method always requires one parameter: the full name of the audio file to be played. This file must be located in the Resources group of your application in Xcode. It cannot be placed on the web server with your HTML, JavaScript, and CSS files. If this file is not included in the application's resources, it is not played.

In this example, bird.mp3 is passed to the `playSound` method of the Device object and is handled as seen in the following code. Notice that the name of the file, `clip`, is appended to the sound command. At this point in PhoneGaps development, `playSound` is the only working method that is passed parameters along with the command. It appears that this will change as the PhoneGap team adds more functionality. For information about the PhoneGap roadmap, see Appendix C, "The PhoneGap Development Roadmap."

```
playSound: function(clip) {
     return Device.exec('sound:' + clip);
}
```

This section showed you how you can activate the device behaviors available via PhoneGap. Section 2 shows the Objective-C portions of the PhoneGap library that support this capability.

Section 2: Objective-C Device Activation

If you are not familiar with Objective-C and how it is used to create iPhone applications, refer to Erica Sadun's book, *The iPhone Developer's Cookbook,* for more information on the Objective-C described in this section. If you just want to use the PhoneGap library to write JavaScript applications for the iPhone, you do not need to read this section.

After the web components, the HTML, CSS, and JavaScript for your application are retrieved from the web server, the iPhone API fires an event that is captured and handled by the `webViewDidStartLoad` method of the `GlassAppDelegate` object. This method, as in the following code, initializes a PhoneGap `Device` object.

```
//when web application loads pass it device information
- (void)webViewDidStartLoad:(UIWebView *)theWebView {
    [theWebView stringByEvaluatingJavaScriptFromString:
                        [[Device alloc] init]];
}
```

The following `init` method of the Device object creates a string that is a series of JavaScript calls. Each of these calls sets a specific global variable. These variables include the model of the device, its unique id, iPhone or iPod Touch, and the version of the device's OS.

After the JavaScript is assembled, it is returned from the `init` method so that it can be used by the `stringByEvaluatingJavaScriptFromString` method of the UIWebView object. By having the UIWebView evaluate the JavaScript string, the global JavaScript variables such as `__gap_device_uniqueid` are set. Later in this chapter, these global variables are assembled into a JavaScript object.

```
@implementation Device


- (NSString *)init{


     jsCallBack = nil;
     myCurrentDevice = [UIDevice currentDevice];
```

```
    return jsCallBack = [[NSString alloc] initWithFormat:@"\
                        __gap = true; \
                        __gap_version='0.1'; \
                        __gap_device_model='%s'; \
                        __gap_device_version='%s';\
                        __gap_device_uniqueid='%s';",
                        [[myCurrentDevice model] UTF8String],
                        [[myCurrentDevice systemVersion] UTF8String],
                        [[myCurrentDevice uniqueIdentifier] UTF8String]
                        ];
}

- (void)dealloc {
    [jsCallBack release];
      [myCurrentDevice release];
      [super dealloc];
}

@end
```

These global variables are set without making a request. Other behaviors require you to write code to trigger the desired behavior.

Using Objective-C to vibrate the iPhone is one of the easiest behaviors to implement. It is done with the following single line of code if you include the AudioToolbox framework in the resources of your project:

```
AudioServicesPlaySystemSound(kSystemSoundID_Vibrate);
```

How can you get the `AudioServicesPlaySystemSound` function to be called when the UIWebView is told to change its location?

The `GlassAppDelegate` implements the `webView:shouldStartLoadWithRequest:navigationType` method. Because the delegate of the embedded UIWebView, called `webView`, is set to be the `GlassAppDelegate` (as shown in the following code and in line 36 of GlassAppDelegate.m), this method is called every time the embedded UIWebView is told to change its location.

```
webView.delegate = self;
```

The basic behavior of the `webView:shouldStartLoadWithRequest:navigationType` function is straightforward. It is designed to enable you to write code that decides whether the new page requested should actually be loaded. The PhoneGap library takes advantage of this decision-making capability to disallow any of the command requests made by the JavaScript calls shown in Section 1 and execute other Objecive-C code.

The `shouldStartLoadWithRequest` method has several parameters that are available for use, which include

- `curWebView`—The UIWebView containing your JavaScript application
- `request`—A NSURLRequest containing the new URL among other items
- `navigationType`—A UIWebViewNavigationType that can be used to determine whether the request is the result of the user selecting a link or whether it was generated as a result of some other action

```
-(BOOL)webView:(UIWebView *)curWebView
   shouldStartLoadWithRequest:(NSURLRequest *)request
navigationType:(UIWebViewNavigationType)navigationType
```

The URL assembled by the `Device.exec` JavaScript method that causes the device to vibrate, `gap:vibrate`, is contained in the `request` object and easily retrieved as a string by passing the `URL` message to it. This message returns an NSURL type object that is then passed the `absoluteString` message. Thus, a NSString pointer representing the URL is obtained.

```
NSString *url = [[request URL] absoluteString];
NSArray *urlArray = [url componentsSeparatedByString:@"?"];
```

In PhoneGap, determine whether the requested URL is relative to the application's URL found in the url.txt file discussed in Chapter 1, "Developing Dashcode and Xcode." If it is not, then the Safari browser is launched displaying the page at the URL. This causes your application to exit because the iPhone enables only one application to run at a time.

The following code retrieves both the current host being requested found in the `url` parameter and the host of the application found in `appURL`. This is done by passing both of these NSURL objects the `host` message.

Lines 3 and 4 send the `rangeOfString` message to the `urlHost` variable. This is similar to using the `indexOf` method of the JavaScript String object. The following code determines whether the value of the application's host can be found in the requested URL.

```
1 NSString* urlHost = [url host];
2 NSString* appHost = [appURL host];
3 NSRange range = [urlHost rangeOfString:appHost
4       options:NSCaseInsensitiveSearch];
5 if (range.location == NSNotFound)
6       [[UIApplication sharedApplication] openURL:url];
7
8 NSString * jsCallBack = nil;
9 NSArray * parts = [urlString
10       componentsSeparatedByString:"];
```

Line 5 checks the result of the `rangeOfString` method to see whether `appHost` was found in `urlHost`. If it was not, then the `openURL` message is sent to the application. Any time this openURL message is passed, your application exits and the appropriate handling application is launched. If a URL starting with `map:` is passed, the iPhone's map application starts and displays the results of the map URL. Other possible types include `http`, which launches Safari; `tel`, which launches the phone dialer; `mailto`, which launches the mail application; and `youtube.com` URLs, which launches the YouTube application. In any case, your application exits.

Lines 9 and 10 split the URL into its component commands and place each of these in an array called `parts`. This `parts` array is then evaluated to determine which command was sent and any parameters it might have.

PhoneGap uses an if-then-else conditional statement to evaluate the `parts` array. Each command activates a different condition. In the following `vibrate` command condition, a Vibrate object is instantiated and passed the `vibrate` message.

```
else if([(NSString *)[parts objectAtIndex:1]
      isEqualToString:@"vibrate"]){
Vibrate *vibration = [[Vibrate alloc] init];
[vibration vibrate];
[vibration release];
NSLog(@"vibrating");
}
```

It is within the Vibrate object's `vibrate` method, found in Vibrate.m, that the `AudioServicesPlaySystemSound(kSystemSoundID_Vibrate);` call is made.

Handling a GPS information request is done differently. This command is handled directly rather than being passed off to an object for handling. Lines 5–7 assemble a string that contains a JavaScript call, which is the `gotLocation(lat, lon)` function found in the gap.js file where `lat` and `lon` are replaced with the current latitude and longitude that have been constantly collected since the application started running.

```
1 if([(NSString *)[parts objectAtIndex:1]
2                  isEqualToString:@"getloc"]){
3             NSLog(@"location request!");
4
5             jsCallBack = [[NSString alloc]
6                   initWithFormat:@"gotLocation('%f','%f');"
7                         , lat, lon];
8             NSLog( %@",jsCallBack);
9             [theWebView
10                   stringByEvaluatingJavaScriptFromString:
11                                     jsCallBack];
12
13             [jsCallBack release];
14 }
```

To cause this JavaScript string `jsCallBack` to execute, the UIWebView passed as the parameter `theWebView` to the `shouldStartLoadWithRequest` function must be sent the `stringByEvaluatingJavaScriptFromString` message with the JavaScript string as its parameter. At this point, the Objective-C portion of the library has completed its task.

The gotLocation JavaScript function now, as shown in the following code, calls the `Device.Location set` method:

```
function gotLocation(lat, lon) {
    return Device.Location.set(lat, lon)
}
```

The `Device.Location.set` method stores the latitude and longitude in the `Device.Location` object and then, if it exists, calls the `callback` function that was described in Section 1. Notice that after the `callback` method is called, line 6 sets the `callback` method to null. This means that each time you request location information, you must set the `callback` method:

```
1 set: function(lat, lon) {
2       Device.Location.lat = lat;
3       Device.Location.lon = lon;
4       if(Device.Location.callback != null) {
5             Device.Location.callback(lat, lon)
6             Device.Location.callback = null;
7       }
8 }
```

If you choose not to set the `callback` method each time you request location information, no callback function is called.

Handling the `sound` command is similar to handling the `getloc` command. The main difference is that no data is needed by the JavaScript portion of the application and so no `stringByEvaluatingJavaScriptFromString` message is sent to the UIWebView. Instead, a Sound object is created much like the code that handles the `vibrate` command.

```
else if ([(NSString *)[parts objectAtIndex:1]
                         isEqualToString:@"sound"]) {
      NSLog(@"playing sound");
      NSLog([parts objectAtIndex:2]);
      NSString *ef = (NSString *)[parts objectAtIndex:2];
      NSArray *soundFile = [ef componentsSeparatedByString:@"."];

      NSString *file = (NSString *)[soundFile objectAtIndex:0];
      NSString *ext = (NSString *)[soundFile objectAtIndex:1];
       NSLog(@"about to allocate %@, %@",file, ext);
       sound = [[Sound alloc] initWithContentsOfFile:
                  [mainBundle pathForResource:file ofType:ext]];
       NSLog(@"sound allocated");
       [sound play];
}
```

This Sound object, found in Sound.m, is initialized with the path to the sound file. This file, as stated in Section 1, must be in the Resources group of your Xcode project. Because the file is in the Resources group, the `mainBundle` object, that represents your installed application, can be sent the `pathForResource:ofType` message that returns the full path to the sound file on the device, as seen on lines 11 and 12 in the previous code. Line 14 sends the play message to the Sound object so that the user hears the sound.

The `initWithContentsOfFile` method of the Sound object shows you how to convert audio files, such as mp3 files, to system sounds. To do this, the audio files must be very short. In fact, Apple suggests that they be less than five seconds long. Each system sound is created using a URL to its location. Line 1 of the following code indicates how to do this with any path string. Line 3 is the one of interest.

```
1 - (id) initWithContentsOfFile:(NSString *)path
2 {
.
.
.
3 NSURL *filePath = [NSURL fileURLWithPath:path
                        isDirectory:NO];
4 AudioServicesCreateSystemSoundID((CFURLRef)filePath,
                &soundID);
.
.
.
5 }
```

Line 4 causes an audio file to be modified to be a system sound. System sounds are different than standard audio file playback in that they are re-interpreted and stored in the OS itself. When it is time to play them, a media player is not needed. The `AudioServicesCreateSystemSoundID` function is called to accomplish this.

Notice that it takes two parameters. The first is the URL to the audio file and the second is a pointer to a SystemSoundID. In this case, the SystemSoundID is the `soundID` attribute of the Sound object, which is used later to play the sound in the Sound object's `play` method.

As shown in the following code, the Sound object's play method consists of one line of code. A media player is not used to play the sound; instead, a call to `AudioServicesPlaySystemSound` is used. When this call is made and passed a SystemSoundID, the user hears the sound.

```
- (void) play {
    AudioServicesPlaySystemSound(soundID);
}
```

Regardless of what sound you want to use for a system sound, the steps for its creation and use are always the same.

1. Get a URL that represents the location of the audio file on the device.
2. Generate the system sound and store its ID.
3. Play the system sound.

In PhoneGap, the system sound is generated each time you request it to be played, which is unnecessary. You could create the system sound once and then play it any number of times.

As mentioned earlier in this section, the GPS hardware is activated in PhoneGap when your application launches. This is accomplished with the first three lines of the `applicationDidFinishLaunching` method code of the GlassAppDelegate. As shown in the following code, these three lines of code intialize a CLLocationManager, store it in the `locationManager` attribute of the GlassAppDelegate class, and tell it to start updating the GPS information.

```
locationManager = [[CLLocationManager alloc] init];
locationManager.delegate = self;
[locationManager startUpdatingLocation];
```

This CLLocationManager is the class that wraps the GPS and WiFi hardware used to determine the device's current location. It uses input from both the GPS chip and any open WiFi access points to determine the current latitude and longitude.

The second line in the previous code tells the `locationManager` object to call the `didUpdateToLocation` of the GlassAppDelegate each time a location change is detected. It does this by setting the delegate of the `locationManager` object to be the current GlassAppDelegate that is represented here as the `self` keyword. For more information on delegates, see Erica Sadun's book *The iPhone Developer's Cookbook* (Chapters 2 and 4).

The delegate method that is called each time a location change is detected is `didUpdateToLocation` and can be found in the GlassAppDelegate.m file. As shown in the following code, it frees any existing stored location and then stores the current location that was passed to the method as the `newLocation` parameter. This stored parameter is used by the `shouldStartLoadWithRequest` in its `getloc` condition as previously shown.

```
-(void)locationManager:(CLLocationManager *)manager
     //Author's note.
     //There is a potential bug here.
     //If the newLocation == lastKnown then
     //the newLocation object is released
      //[newLocation retain] should be called
      //before [lastKnownLoation release]
     //The code shown here is as it ships in the
     //PhoneGap product.
      didUpdateToLocation:(CLLocation *)newLocation
      fromLocation:(CLLocation *)oldLocation
{
      [lastKnownLocation release];
      lastKnownLocation = newLocation;
      [lastKnownLocation retain];
}
```

The activation of the accelerometers is handled in much the same way as the activation of the GPS hardware. The three lines in the following code tell the accelerometers to store the acceleration information every 1/40 of a second and then sets the accelerometer's delegate to be the current GlassAppDelegate object like it is for the location manager.

```
 [[UIAccelerometer sharedAccelerometer]
          setUpdateInterval:1.0/40.0];
[[UIAccelerometer sharedAccelerometer] setDelegate:self];
```

In this case, the called method is not `didUpdateToLocation` but `didAccelerate`.

As shown in the following code, the `didAccelerate` method is much like the `didUpdateToLocation` method. It retrieves the accelerometer information, but instead of storing it locally on the Objective-C side of the library, it sends it to the JavaScript side much like the handling of the `gotloc` command seen earlier in this section.

```
-(void) accelerometer:(UIAccelerometer *)accelerometer
      didAccelerate:(UIAcceleration *)acceleration {
            NSString * jsCallBack = nil;
            NSLog(@"accelerating");
            jsCallBack = [[NSString alloc]
                  initWithFormat:
                  @"gotAcceleration('%f','%f','%f');",
                  acceleration.x,
                  acceleration.y,
                  acceleration.z];
      [webView
      stringByEvaluatingJavaScriptFromString:jsCallBack];
}
```

Although other commands are handled in the `shouldStartLoadWithRequest` method, none of them worked at the time of this writing, so they were not covered. The items covered in this section currently work and are available in the Xcode template installer for PhoneGap applications.

Summary

This chapter showed you how to activate a few desirable features of iPhone or iPod Touch devices from within your JavaScript application using the PhoneGap library. Using features such as GPS location, accelerometer values, phone vibration, and sounds increases the richness of your application.

Reviewing the examples included in the PGDeviceCatalog and working in Objective-C should enable you to add additional features such as scanning the Bonjour network for nearby devices, adding, removing, and retrieving contacts from the contacts application or any other built-in behavior that is available to Objective-C applications.

Using the approach described in this chapter, your JavaScript application can do most anything a pure Objective-C application can do.

6

Embedding Google Maps

One capability often needed in iPhone applications is the use of maps. There are several ways to display maps from closing the application and launching the standard iPhone Map application to using a standard Google map. Both approaches have limitations. This chapter discusses how to create and use a Google-based map that looks and behaves like the iPhone Map application without closing the application.

Section 1: Displaying a Map from Within Your QuickConnect JavaScript Application

The iPhone enables an engineer or programmer to use maps with hybrid applications in a couple of ways. The simplest way is to add a link in the display that begins with http://maps.google.com and contains the mapping information desired. When the user selects such a link, the application exits, and the standard map application launches displaying the requested map.

This approach is simple to use and quick to create. The drawback is that your application closes, which is generally considered bad software design. The application ends up having a cobbled together feeling and the user usually desires a more integrated approach.

Another drawback is that although Google can respond to requests such as "pizza" and drop multiple pins, it is not currently possible to drop multiple pins in specific locations you define. For example, when creating an application, you might want to drop pins at places in town. If these places do not have searchable groupings such as "pizza," it is not possible to specify multiple pin locations with descriptions in a URL request sent to Google. This limitation can be frustrating if you want to use latitudes and longitudes of the locations on which a pin is to be dropped.

Another approach is to do essentially the same thing in your application that you would do in a standard web page. In this case, use Google's AJAX API to embed a map in a div in the displayed HTML. You can then continue to use Google's JavaScript API to place each pin independently.

Although this approach enables you to keep the user in your application, it also has drawbacks. First, the UIWebView displaying your map doesn't enable scrolling within divs. The touch and move events are handled at a lower level and are not sent to the Google-provided JavaScript that interacts with the embedded map. This means that you can display the map but won't be able to change the map's displayed location.

Another drawback is the size of Google's standard location information bubbles. They are sized for displaying in a browser on a full-sized machine. When a bubble displays on the iPhone, it tends to fill a good portion of the map. Most of the bubble usually displays off screen and is therefore unreadable because of the scrolling problem mentioned previously. Although it is possible to resize the content of these types of bubbles, it is not possible to resize standard Google bubbles.

Obviously, it is more optimal to embed the map in the application and show multiple pins as in the second option but have the scrolling and display capabilities of the first option. The QuickConnectiPhone framework has a component that enables you to do this by making a single JavaScript call.

The MapExample Xcode project shows how this is done. Download this project from http://sourceforge.net/projects/quickconnect/ as part of the QuickConnectiPhone zip file. The MapExample project is found in the Examples directory.

The main screen of this example consists of a single displayed HTML button, as shown in Figure 6.1. The button's `onclick` listener is set to be the `showTheMap` function found in the project's main.js file and is shown in the following code. It sets up three locations: Rexburg, Idaho; Wyoming; a wilderness area.

```
function showTheMap(event)
{
    //a location consists of a latitude,
    //a longitude, and a description
    var locationsArray = new Array();
    rexburg = new Array();
    rexburg.push(43.82211);
    rexburg.push(-111.76860);
    rexburg.push("County Court House");
    locationsArray.push(rexburg);

    var wyoming = new Array();
    wyoming.push(42.86);
    wyoming.push(-109.45);
    wyoming.push("Wyoming   Place");
    locationsArray.push(wyoming);

    var wilderness = new Array();
    wilderness.push(45.35);
    wilderness.push(-115);
    wilderness.push("River  of No Return Wilderness");
    locationsArray.push(wilderness);

    var sandwichShop = new Array();
```

Figure 6.1 Main screen of the MapExample application showing the HTML button

```
    sandwichShop.push(42.86);
    sandwichShop.push(-112.45);
    sandwichShop.push("Somewhere Sandwiches");
    locationsArray.push(sandwichShop);

    showMap(event, locationsArray);
}
```

Each location is an array that consists of three elements: latitude, longitude, and a short description to be displayed for each pin placed. These locations are added to the `locationsArray`. Although the order of the values added to each location is fixed, the `locationsArray` itself is order-independent.

In an actual application, the values used for each location might be stored in a database, retrieved from an RSS feed, or some other location. You can even retrieve them during the run of your application. If you know street addresses, use Google's geocoding JavaScript API to get their latitudes and longitudes, http://code.google.com/apis/maps/documentation/services.html#Geocoding_Object. At runtime, this is slow. It is better to get the latitudes and longitudes for locations of interest using a batch process at design time and then store them prior to shipping the application.

After creating a JavaScript array containing all the required locations, it is passed to the framework's `showMap` function along with the event that causes the call to the `showTheMap` function. At this point, the framework takes over and using the `makeCall` function described in Chapter 4, "GPS Acceleration and Other Native Functions with QuickConnect," it instructs the Objective-C portion of the framework to display a map with pins placed at each location, as shown in Figure 6.2.

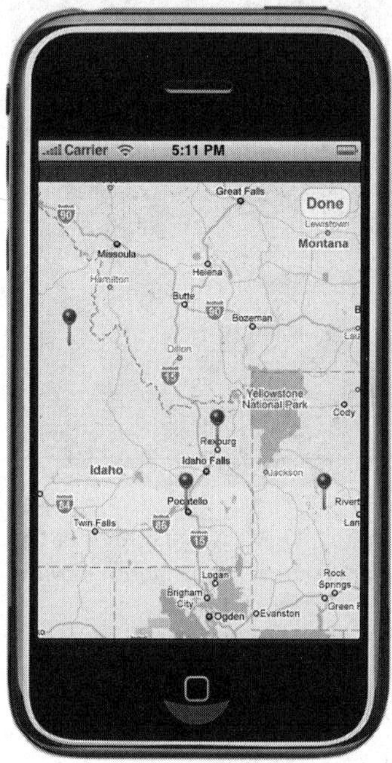

Figure 6.2 The MapExample application displaying a pin for each location

The framework displays the map in an Objective-C MapView object. This MapView class, described in Section 2, enables the user to use touch and swipe gestures to control the map as in Apple's Map application. By double touching a location on the map, it centers and zooms on that location. The user can also double touch a pin to center the map and zoom in on the touched pin.

When the user single touches a pin, a short description displays in a small black box, much like in the map application shown in Figure 6.3. If the user touches and drags a pin, it relocates to the new position on the map.

When the user no longer needs the map, he selects the Done button, and the MapView disappears. The application's view displays in the same state as when the application displayed the map. This solves the usability and resumed state problems caused by

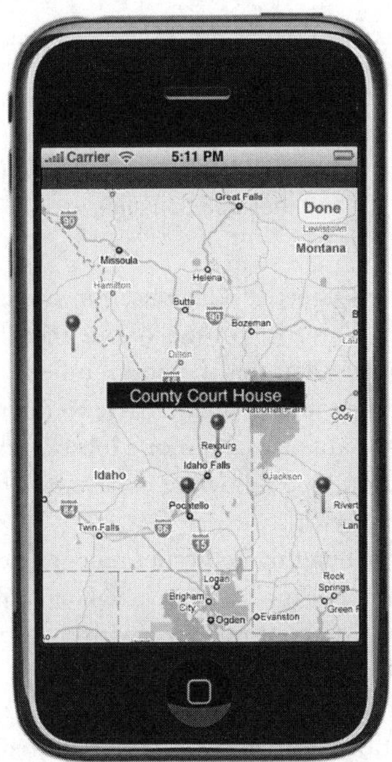

Figure 6.3 The MapExample application displaying a short description

closing the application, launching the Map application, closing the map application, and then relaunching the application.

By making calls to the `showMap` JavaScript function of the framework, your application has built-in maps. Section 2 shows in detail how the Objective-C MapView and other classes of the framework are designed and used.

Section 2: Objective-C Implementation of the QuickConnect Mapping Module

The QuickConnect mapping module consists of three classes:

`MapView`—The main display element containing the map images

`Pin`—A custom pin to be displayed at a location

`InfoWindow`—A class used to display a short description associated with a specific pin

Figure 6.4 shows the relationships among these classes. Each `MapView` can have many `Pins`, and each `Pin` must have at least one `MapView`. There is also a one-to-one relationship between `Pins` and `InfoWindows`. In other words, for each `Pin`, there must be one `InfoWindow`; for each `InfoWindow`, there must be one `Pin`.

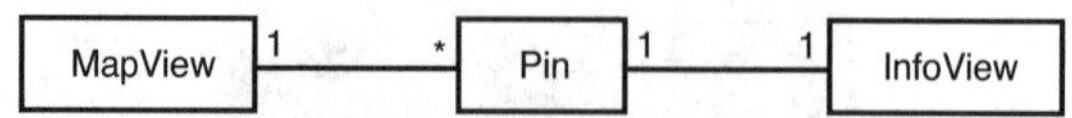

Figure 6.4 The classes in the mapping module and their relationships

Being modular in nature, an Objective-C application needs to interact directly with the MapView class and its API. This API consists of one method: `initWithFrame:andLocations`. When this method is called, a map is generated, pins are placed on the map, and short descriptions are available to the user when touching a pin. In addition to this, if the user double taps a pin or a location on the map, the map zooms and centers itself on that location. The following code shows how this MapView API is used in the QuickConnect framework.

As with the GPS location, debugging and other requests described in Chapter 2, "JavaScript Modularity and iPhone Applications," a call to display an embedded map uses the front controller and application controllers. As with those pieces of functionality, a `showMap` command is associated with the `showMapVCO` via the QCCommandMappings.m file. The `doCommand` method of this VCO is small and mainly consists of placing the latitudes, longitudes, and descriptions sent with the JavaScript request in an array by themselves. This is done by skipping the first element of the parameters array because it is the `QuickConnectViewController` for your application. The `doCommand` method, shown in the following code, is found in the MapExample Xcode project, which can be downloaded from http://sourceforge.net/projects/QuickConnect.

```
+ (id) doCommand:(NSArray*) parameters{
    NSRange aRange = NSMakeRange(1, [parameters count]-1);
      NSArray *locations = [parameters subarrayWithRange:aRange];
    //size the MapView to fill the screen
      MapView *aMapView = [[MapView alloc] initWithFrame:[[UIScreen mainScreen]
applicationFrame]
            andLocations:locations];
    QuickConnectViewController *theController =
            [parameters objectAtIndex:0];
    //add the map view to the application's main view
    [[[theController webView]
            superview] addSubview:aMapView];
      return nil;
}
```

Because the `QuickConnectViewController` has a reference to the `UIWebView` that displays and runs your application, it can be used to obtain a pointer to the main application view. This is done by sending the `superview` message to the `UIWebView`. The new `MapView` is then added to the main application view by passing it as a parameter with the `addSubview` message. When this message is sent, the `MapView` appears and fills the screen hiding the display of the `UIWebView`.

Because the MapView functionality is a self-contained module, it is easily re-usable in many different applications (see Chapter 2 for a discussion of modularity). It can even be used in hybrid Macintosh applications with minor, internal modifications for map display.

All Google maps, regardless of what displays, are web pages. Therefore, the `MapView` object has an attribute that is its own `UIWebView` called `webMapView`. It is not the same UIWebView instance that displays your application.

This `webMapView`, as shown in the following code, displays the mapView.html file found in the Resouces MapView group and its delegate is set to the MapView class. The MapView group contains both an embeddable UIView and a WebViewDelegate that handles all the events for the UIWebView.

```
(id)initWithFrame:(CGRect)frame
          andLocations:(NSArray*)aLocationList {
    if (self = [super initWithFrame:frame]) {
          OKToTouch = NO;
          self.locations = aLocationList;
          frame.origin.y -= 20;
          UIWebView *aWebView = [[UIWebView alloc]
initWithFrame:frame];
          self.webMapView = aWebView;
           [aWebView release];

           aWebView.userInteractionEnabled = NO;
           //set the web view delegate
//for the web view to be itself
           [aWebView setDelegate:self];

           //determine the path to the mapView.html file
//in the Resources directory
           NSString *filePathString = [[NSBundle mainBundle]
pathForResource:@"mapView" ofType:@"html"];
           MESSAGE(@"%@", filePathString);
           //build the URL and the request for the
//mapView.html file
           NSURL *aURL = [NSURL fileURLWithPath:filePathString];
           NSURLRequest *aRequest =
[NSURLRequest requestWithURL:aURL];

           //load the mapView.html file into the web view.
           [aWebView loadRequest:aRequest];

           //add the web view to the content view
           [self addSubview:self.webMapView];
    }
```

```
33        return self;
34 }
```

Some might think that for reasons of simplicity, the `MapView` class is not needed. This is not the case. Because the `UIWebView` consumes all touch events and does not enable such events to be consumed by the HTML elements it displays, the scrolling issue described in Section 1 occurs.

To solve this problem, line 12 of the previous code turns off all event consumption by the contained `UIWebView`. This enables the containing `MapView` object to consume all the events as its delegate. The delegate then becomes responsible for indicating to the `UIWebView` that the page it contains should be scrolled.

To scroll a map, determine that a touch moved after it started. To accomplish this, the `MapView`'s standard `touchesMoved:withEvent` method must be implemented.

```
-(void)touchesMoved:(NSSet *)touches
            withEvent:(UIEvent *)event{
    if(OKToTouch){
        if([touches count] == 1){
            UITouch *touch = [touches anyObject];
            CGPoint prevLoc =
                [touch previousLocationInView:self];
            CGPoint curLoc =
                [touch locationInView:self];
            double touchDeltaX = curLoc.x - prevLoc.x;
            double touchDeltaY = curLoc.y - prevLoc.y;

            NSString *javaScriptCall =
                [[NSString alloc]
                    initWithFormat:@"scroll(%f, %f)"
                    ,touchDeltaX, touchDeltaY];
            NSString *result = [webMapView
                stringByEvaluatingJavaScriptFromString
                        javaScriptCall];

            if([result compare:@"true"] == 0){
                int numPins = [pins count];
                for(int i = 0; i < numPins; i++){
                        Pin *aPin =
                            [pins objectAtIndex:i];
                    [aPin moveX:touchDeltaX
                            andY:touchDeltaY];
          [aPin.info moveX:touchDeltaX
                            andY:touchDeltaY];
                }
            }
        }
```

```
        else if([touches count] == 2){
            //pinch
        }
    }
}
```

This implementation of `touchesMoved:withEvent` first determines how much the touch has moved. It does this by finding the difference, the delta, between the current event location and the location of the previous event and then passing this difference to the HTML page in the `webMapView`. To do this, the `stringByEvaluatingJavaSCriptFromString` message is sent with a JavaScript function call to `scroll`.

This JavaScript `scroll` function, shown in the following code and in the map.js file of the Resouces MapView group, uses the JavaScript Google map API to recenter the viewable map. It does this by applying the required change in the x and y values to the map's current center, and then it notifies the map object to center itself on this new location.

```
function scroll(deltaX, deltaY){
    try{
        var centerPoint = map.fromLatLngToDivPixel(map.getCenter());
        centerPoint.x -= deltaX;
        centerPoint.y -= deltaY;
        var centerLatLng =
            map.fromDivPixelToLatLng(centerPoint);
        map.setCenter(centerLatLng);
    }
    catch(error){
        return false;
    }
    return true;
}
```

When this JavaScript function successfully completes, it returns true so that the remainder of the `touchesMoved:withEvent` method can tell each of the displayed pins to also change its location.

Because the underlying UIWebView's consumption, in order to implement map scrolling, is turned off, standard Google map pins cannot detect that they have been touched. Because of this inability, the standard Google map description bubbles cannot be displayed and hidden for these pins. Thus, it becomes necessary to create a custom `Pin` class.

This class, found in the Classes:MapView grouping, uses the pinInserted.png image for its display. The `Pin` class uses this file in Resources:Images for its visual display; it can easily be replaced with any image file you choose.

An object of the `Pin` class is initialized for each location your application sends from the JavaScript side. To do this, the `initWithFrame:andImage:andLocation` method shown in the following code is called. It creates a `UIImageView` for the pin's image, sets the pin's location, and turns on consumption of events by setting its userInteractionEnabled attribute to true.

```
-(id)initWithFrame:(CGRect)frame
        andImage:(NSString*)anImage
        andLocation:(MapViewLocation)aLocation{

    if (self = [super initWithFrame:frame]) {
            UIImageView *pinImage = [[UIImageView alloc]
            initWithImage:[UIImage imageNamed:anImage]];
            [self addSubview:pinImage];
            [pinImage release];
            location = aLocation;
            self.userInteractionEnabled = YES;
            self.backgroundColor = [UIColor clearColor];
     }
     return self;
}
```

By enabling a Pin object's user interaction, it becomes possible for the pinto trap and consume events. If a pin is touched, the touchesBegan:withEvent method of the Pin object is called and used to modify the display.

The implementation of this function is found in Pin.m and shown in the following code. It checks to ensure that the current and previous events have the same location on the screen. This check ensures that the code in this method is not executed if the user drags his finger on the screen in a swipe-like motion.

Assuming that no swiping occurs, two situations are handled by touchesBegan:withEvent. The first is if the user single taps the pin. In this case, the desired behavior is to display the simple message sent along with the location from the JavaScript side of the application. To accomplish this, Objective-C's reflection capabilities are used to pass a singleTouch message to the pin itself.

The performSelector:withObject:afterDelay message is sent to the pin rather than making a call directly. This allows for differentiation between a single and double tap. As shown on line 13, the user has .4 seconds to complete a double tap. If the double tap doesn't happen, the first touch is consumed and the second touch is treated as distinct from it.

If, on the other hand, the user double taps the pin within the .4 second time limit, a cancelPreviousPerformRequestsWithTarget:selector:object message is passed to stop the passing of the singleTouch message. This delay/execute or cancel approach is the standard method for detecting the number of taps for touches.

In this case, if a single tap is detected, the singleTouch message is passed and the pin's short description is displayed. If a double tap is detected, the map is zoomed and centered on the location of the pin.

```
1 -(void)touchesBegan:(NSSet *)touches
2            withEvent:(UIEvent *)event{
```

```
    UITouch *touch = [touches anyObject];
      CGPoint prevLoc = [touch previousLocationInView:self];
      CGPoint curLoc = [touch locationInView:self];

      if(CGPointEqualToPoint(prevLoc, curLoc)){
        NSUInteger tapCount = [touch tapCount];
        switch (tapCount) {
              case 1:
                  [self performSelector:
                                   @selector(singleTouch)
                         withObject:nil afterDelay:.4];
                  break;
              case 2:
                  [NSObject cancelPreviousPerformRequestsWithTarget:self
                         selector:@selector(singleTouch)
                         object:nil];
                  //zoom and center on this pin
                  MESSAGE(@"double tap pin %i, %i",
                         location.x, location.y);

                  double latOffset =
(location.y+42)/((MapView*)self.superview).pixelsPerDegLatitude;
                  double lngOffset =
(location.x+10)/((MapView*)self.superview).pixelsPerDegLongitude;
                  double latitude = [[((MapView*)self.superview).northWest
objectAtIndex:0] doubleValue] - latOffset;
                  double longitude = [[((MapView*)self.superview).northWest
objectAtIndex:1] doubleValue] + lngOffset;
                  MESSAGE(@"latitude: %f longitude: %f northWest: %@",
                        latitude,
                        longitude,
                        ((MapView*)self.superview).northWest);
                  NSString *javaScriptCall = [[NSString alloc]
initWithFormat:@"zoomTo(%f, %f)",latitude, longitude];
                  NSString *mapDescription =
[((MapView*)self.superview).webMapView
stringByEvaluatingJavaScriptFromString:javaScriptCall];

                  [((MapView*)self.superview)
setMapLatLngFrameWithDescription:mapDescription];
                  [((MapView*)self.superview) updatePinLocations];

                  break;
              default:
                  break;
          }
      }
}
```

By enabling zooming and centering on a double touch of either a pin or the map there is an increase in usability of your application. The standard map application does not center when either of these items is double touched; it just zooms in. If the user executes a double touch, he usually needs to follow this up with a swipe to display the region around the area of interest. The application does not have this limitation.

You can also move pins in the map by dragging them. This is accomplished by the `touchesMoved:withEvent` method shown in the following code and is like the map scrolling shown previously. One difference is that a `cancelPreviousPerformRequestsWithTarget:selector:object` message is passed again to avoid the display of the short description because the `touchesBegan` method is called prior to `touchesMoved`. If a cancellation message is not sent, the short message is displayed and the pin is moved. This creates a poor user experience.

```
1 -(void)touchesMoved:(NSSet *)touches
2               withEvent:(UIEvent *)event{
3       if([touches count] == 1){
4
5         [NSObject cancelPreviousPerformRequestsWithTarget:self selector:@selec-
tor(singleTouch) object:nil];
6         moved = YES;
7             UITouch *touch = [touches anyObject];
8             CGPoint prevLoc = [touch previousLocationInView:self];
9             CGPoint curLoc = [touch locationInView:self];
10             double touchDeltaX = curLoc.x - prevLoc.x;
11             double touchDeltaY = curLoc.y - prevLoc.y;
12             [self moveX:touchDeltaX andY:touchDeltaY];
13          MapViewLocation mapLoc = self.location;
14          mapLoc.x += touchDeltaX;
15          mapLoc.y += touchDeltaY;
16          self.location = mapLoc;
17          if(self.info != nil){
18              self.info.hidden = TRUE;
19              self.info.label.text = @"Unknown";
20          }
21      }
22 }
```

Much like the map scrolling, the movement of a pin uses the previous and current locations to update a location. In the map scrolling case, the location is the center of the map. In the pin moving case, the location being updated is the upper-left display point of the pin and its latitude and longitude.

Because the pin no longer represents the map location originally specified, the short description originally supplied and associated with this pin is probably invalid. It is therefore set to `Unknown`. Additionally, if the short message displays when the user drags the pin, it is closed to reduce the CPU requirements of drawing both the pin and the message as they are moved. This is accomplished by line 18.

The info attribute of the Pin class is used to display the short description supplied by the JavaScript portion of your application. It is an InfoWindow object that is itself a UIView and has a single attribute: label.

The initWithFrame:andDescription method of InfoWindow, shown in the following code and in the InfoWindow.m file found in Classes:MapView, shows the setting of the location in the window of the viewable description as well as its content. The user interface item used to display the short description is a UILabel.

```
-(id)initWithFrame:(CGRect)frame


andDescription:(NSString*)description{
      if (self = [super initWithFrame:frame]) {
        [self setBackgroundColor:[UIColor blackColor]];
        CGRect labelFrame = CGRectMake(0, 0,
                                       frame.size.width,
                                       frame.size.height);
            label = [[UILabel alloc]
                       initWithFrame:labelFrame];
        label.text = description;
        label.backgroundColor = [UIColor clearColor];
        label.textColor = [UIColor whiteColor];
        label.textAlignment = UITextAlignmentCenter;
        [self addSubview:label];
        [label release];
      }
      return self;
}
```

By using a UILabel to display the short description, you receive a whole host of capabilities. You can now set the font, its alignment, size, color, and many other attributes such as shadows. It is possible to draw the text directly instead of using a UILabel, but this uses more lines of code. By using a prebuilt UILabel, you have a much more supportable application.

The three classes—MapView, Pin, and InfoWindow—make up the MapView module. They contain all the source code required to show a basic Google map, but they can easily be modified to exhibit more complex behavior.

For example, a modification can be made to the InfoWindow class so that it displays more detail either by changing its display size or by displaying another complete UIView, such as Apple's standard map application. Or the MapView class can be modified to retrieve driving directions such as the standard application. Although both modifications require knowledge of Objective-C, they are not technically difficult.

Another item of interest not yet covered is how to adjust the locations of all of the Pin objects and their InfoWindows while scrolling or zooming the map. Each of these classes has a moveX:andY method. These methods have as parameters the number of pixels in the x and y directions to shift the pin or information window and is shown in the following code.

A novice Objective-C programmer might attempt to modify the location by using a line of code, such as `[self frame].origin.x += xChange`. This line of code throws no exceptions, causes no compilation errors, and does not change the location of the `Pin` or `InfoWindow`.

In Objective-C `UIView` classes, such as the `Pins` and `InfoWindow`, the frame representing the top-left location and the width and height is applied only in two instances. The first is if it is initialized with the `initWithFrame` message. In this case, the frame structure included as a parameter is used to size the view. The second is when the frame attribute is swapped out for another, as shown in the `moveX:andY` method.

```
- (void) moveX:(double) xChange andY:(double)yChange{
      CGRect frame = [self frame];
      frame.origin.x += xChange;
      frame.origin.y += yChange;
      self.frame = frame;
}
```

Because of this limited changeability, a direct manipulation of a view's frame attribute has no effect.

The `moveX:andY` method needs to be called every time the map is scrolled or zoomed. In the `touchesMoved:withEvent` method of the `MapView` class, every pin is sent this message for each event that is captured.

```
for(int i = 0; i < numPins; i++){
      Pin *aPin = [pins objectAtIndex:i];
      [aPin moveX:touchDeltaX andY:touchDeltaY];
[aPin.info moveX:touchDeltaX andY:touchDeltaY];
}
```

Map zooming is handled in the `touchesEnded:withEvent` method of the `MapView` class. This message is passed by the device to a `MapView` object after all `touchesBegan` and `touchesMoved` messages have been handled.

In the following code, notice that after determining that the touch consists of two taps, the location in the map of the touch is determined. This is followed by a call to the JavaScript function `zoomTo` as shown previously in the Pin `zoom` example.

```
-(void)touchesEnded:(NSSet *)touches
        withEvent:(UIEvent *)event{

        if(OKToTouch){
              UITouch *touch = [touches anyObject];
              if ([touch tapCount] == 2){
                    //zoom and center
                    CGPoint curLoc = [touch locationInView:self];

                     double latOffset = curLoc.y/self.pixelsPerDegLatitude;
                     double lngOffset = curLoc.x/pixelsPerDegLongitude;
```

```
12
13                  double latitude = [[northWest objectAtIndex:0] doubleValue] -
latOffset;
14                  double longitude = [[northWest objectAtIndex:1] doubleValue]
+ lngOffset;
15                  NSString *javaScriptCall = [[NSString alloc]
initWithFormat:@"zoomTo(%f, %f)",latitude, longitude];
16                  NSString *mapDescription = [webMapView
stringByEvaluatingJavaScriptFromString:javaScriptCall];
17
18                  [self setMapLatLngFrameWithDescription:mapDescription];
19                  [self updatePinLocations];
20            }
21            else{
22                  NSLog(@"touched");
23            }
24      }
25 }
```

After accomplishing the zoom, for either `Pin` and `MapView` objects' double taps, an `updatePinLocations` message is passed to the `MapView` object, as shown on line 19 in the previous code. As shown in the following code, that call causes the location of each pin to be updated based on the latitude and longitude of each pin as well as the amount the map has been zoomed.

This zoom scale is represented by the pixelsPerDegLatitude and pixelsPerDeg-Longitude attributes of the MapView class set in a previous call to the `setMapLatLngFrameWithDescription` method.

```
-(void) updatePinLocations{
      int numPins = [pins count];
      for(int i = 0; i < numPins; i++){
            Pin *aPin = (Pin*)[pins objectAtIndex:i];
            double latitudeDelta = [[northWest objectAtIndex:0] doubleValue] -
aPin.location.latitude;
            double longitudeDelta =  aPin.location.longitude - [[northWest
objectAtIndex:1] doubleValue];

            double yPixels = latitudeDelta * pixelsPerDegLatitude;
            double xPixels = longitudeDelta * pixelsPerDegLongitude;
            MapViewLocation aPinLocation = aPin.location;
            aPinLocation.x = xPixels - 10 - 4;
            //the visual pin is ten pixels into the image
            //from the left
            aPinLocation.y = yPixels - 42 + 10;
            //the visual pin is 10 pixels into the image
            //from the bottom

            CGRect pinFrame = aPin.frame;
```

```
19              pinFrame.origin.x = aPinLocation.x;
20              pinFrame.origin.y = aPinLocation.y;
21              aPin.frame = pinFrame;
22              aPin.location = aPinLocation;
23
24              CGRect infoFrame = aPin.info.frame;
25              infoFrame.origin.x = aPinLocation.x - 100;
26              infoFrame.origin.y = aPinLocation.y - 30;
27              aPin.info.frame = infoFrame;
28         }
29 }
```

As in the `moveX:andY` method, the frame needs to be retrieved, modified, and then reset. This is done on lines 18–22 in the previous code for the pin and lines 24–27 for the `Pin` object's associated `InfoWindow`.

Each `Pin` and `InfoWindow` object's location is updated for each zoom. It is possible that some of them will no longer be visible within the bounds of the current MapView, which is not an issue. They are rendered in the nonviewable space outside the screen. The code does not need to hide them.

Summary

This chapter showed you how to embed Google maps into your application and how the map viewing module was created. It also showed you how to manipulate the locations of both custom and standard views.

By making judicious use of calls to the JavaScript in a Google map displayed in a UIWebView, the Google JavaScript API can be used for zooming and centering.

All of this is included in the QuickConnect framework so that you can make one call in JavaScript to display a fully usable Google map. Although easy to use, from the JavaScript side of the framework, it is also easy to use the mapping module in any iPhone Objective-C application you choose to write. In fact, writing just a few lines of code is all that is required.

Custom, embedded Google maps are now within the realm of possibility for your iPhone applications. Version 3.0 of the iPhone OS will make this even easier.

7

Database Access

Most JavaScript-based applications require a web server to store data. With iPhone OS 2.0 or later and the UIWebView class, you can store data on the iPhone without any network access. This means that the application you create is a first-class citizen on the iPhone. This chapter shows you how to store and retrieve data and create databases and tables. This chapter provides you with an easy-to-use JavaScript wrapper for the SQLite database used on the iPhone. The first sections show you how to start using the database. The later sections discuss how to understand the code used in the wrapper.

Section 1: BrowserDBAccess Example Application

The BrowserDBAccess example was created to help you understand how databases can be used in JavaScript applications. It is found in the Examples directory of the QuickConnectFamily folder you can download from http://*sourceforge.net/projects/quickconnect/*.

This example application creates a SQLite database called sampleDB that has one table, `score`. This database exists in the UIWebView and enables the user to query it for information. Databases created in this way are resident on the machine between runs of the application, even though they were not installed with the application. Because of this, if you store data in the database, it is there when the application runs again. Figure 7.1 shows this sample application running before a query is sent to the database.

The score table in the BrowserDBAccess application consists of two fields. The first is a character-based primary key called `player_name`. The second is an integer field called `score`. The primary key field is not autoincrementing, so it must be supplied with a value each time a record is inserted. The BrowserDBAccess application uses several prebuilt JavaScript classes, methods, and functions to access data in the sampleDB database.

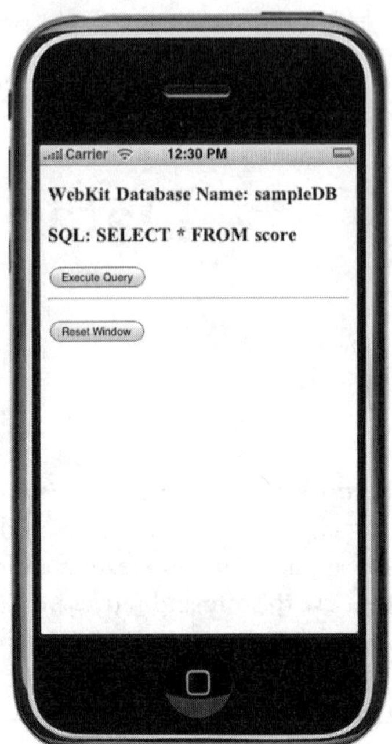

Figure 7.1 The BrowserDBAccess application before the query is executed

Databases, Databases Everywhere

Databases use their own unique vocabulary. Tables are used as groupings for like items. Each of these similar items is called a record. Records consist of values entered into what are referred to as fields. Fields are defined by their name and type. If you think of records as rows in a spreadsheet and fields as columns, you won't be too far off. Tables are similar to sheets. If you add a new record to a dogs table in a database, it is similar to adding a new row to a dogs spreadsheet. It's not the same, but it's close enough to help us understand.

A primary key is something that uniquely identifies a specific record in a table. This can be an integer or text, but there can be no duplicates. A primary key is something similar to a combination of your user name and password for the Apple Developer Connection. Obviously, it would be horrendous if two people had the same login.

A foreign key is another item all together. They are used to link data from two tables together. Imagine two tables, owners and dogs. The owners table has a primary key for each record. To know which dog belongs to which owner, a foreign key is included in the dog table. This foreign key contains the primary key of the owner in the owners table. This is like the registration number of the tag a dog wears on its collar that can track the owner of the dog down if it ends up in the pound.

Section 2: Using WebView SQLite Databases

Sometimes, using a database can seem intimidating. A programmer or engineer needs to keep in mind a myriad of potential pitfalls when storing or retrieving information. Too often, these potential pitfalls prevent programmers from using databases for simple data storage.

On the iPhone, the native way of storing data in and for applications is to use the embedded SQLite database rather than a text or binary file. The ability to quickly and easily use this database engine can determine the success of your applications. To speed up development, a JavaScript class is included in the QuickConnectiPhone framework so that you don't have to worry about the problems associated with using databases.

The DataAccessObject.js file, which is found in the QCiPhone group in both the Dashcode and Xcode templates, contains a wrapper around the code required to access the SQLite database. This JavaScript file is automatically included in the index.html file of your application by both the Xcode and Dashcode templates. This wrapper, the DataAccessObject class, consists of a constructor and four methods, as shown in Table 7.1.

Table 7.1 **The DataAccessObject API**

Attribute/ Method	Return	Description	Parameters
DataAccessObject(dbName, dbVersion, dbDescription, dbSize)	DataAccessObject	Creates a DataAccessObject when called with the new key word.	dbName—A unique identifying string used to reference the specific database. dbVersion—A string that is usually in the form of a floating-point number. dbDescription—A string stating the purpose of the database. dbSize—The minimum amount of disk space allocated to the database in bytes. If null or nothing is passed the default value is equivalent to 5 megabytes.
getData(SQL, parameterArray)	none	A method used to retrieve information based on the SQL passed in from a database created in the UIWebView.	SQL—A valid SQL command string. parameterArray—An array of values used if the SQL command is a prepared statement.
setData(SQL, parameterArray)	None	A method used to store information based on the SQL passed into a database created in the UIWebView.	SQL—A valid SQL command string. parameterArray—An array of values used if the SQL command is a prepared statement.

Table 7.1 **The DataAccessObject API**

Attribute/ Method	Return	Description	Parameters
getNativeData(SQL, parameterArray)	None	A method used to retrieve information based on the SQL passed in from a database installed with the applica-	SQL—A valid SQL command string. parameterArray—An array of values used if the SQL command is a prepared statement.
setNativeData(SQL, parameterArray)	None	A method used to store information based on the SQL passed in to a database installed with the applica-	SQL—A valid SQL command string. parameterArray—An array of values used if the SQL command is a prepared statement.

This JavaScript wrapper class is used in the databaseDefinition.js file included by the templates in your application. databaseDefinition.js is where you state what database or databases your application uses.

The following code, taken from the databaseDefinition.js file of the BrowserDBAccess example application, shows how the constructor is used to create a database that is handled by the WebKit engine used in hybrid iPhone applications. The use of the engine's builtin database support is appropriate when all of the data needed is generated by the application after it is installed.

```
var sampleDatabase = new DataAccessObject("sampleDB", "1.0", "a sample data-
base", 2000);
```

The previous code creates or opens, if it already exists, a database called sampleDB. Because the WebKit engine handles the creation and use of this database, it needs a few pieces of information. The first is the version number for the database. It can be set to any value you prefer; here, it is set to `1.0`. The database is also initialized with a maximum size of `2000` bytes. You can choose to size your database as seems appropriate.

The return value of the previous constructor call is a DataAccessObject that is connected to the underlying SQLite database and is ready for use. Modification of the database is now possible and an example of this is found in the code that follows. It shows the use of the DataAccessObject's `setData` method.

```
sampleDatabase.setData("CREATE TABLE IF NOT EXISTS score ('player_name' VARCHAR
PRIMARY KEY, 'score' INTEGER);");
```

This SQL is for the creation of a table, but the `setData` method is used for all SQL requests that modify database tables, insert or remove data, or change the database in any way.

As described in Chapter 2, "JavaScript Modularity and iPhone Applications," one use of Business Control Functions (BCF) is to get data from the database. The BCF `getScoresBCF` (shown in the following code) does this; it is found in the functions.js file of either example.

This BCF uses the DataAccessObjects' `getData` method to retrieve the records from the `score` table. Line 3 shows the actual `getData` call.

```
1 function getScoresBCF(parameters){
2    var SQL = 'SELECT * FROM score';
3   sampleDatabase.getData(SQL);
4 }
```

Figure 7.2 shows the data retrieved using this BCF. Note that the `getScoresBCF` returns nothing because the `getData` method is asynchronous. Because it is asynchronous, it does not return the sql query's resultant data. The QuickConnectiPhone framework handles the receipt of the data and passes it to any other control objects you mapped to the same command as the BCF. The `displayScoresVCF` View Control Function in the functions.js file is mapped to the same command as `getScoresBCF`, so the framework passes the information to it when it becomes available.

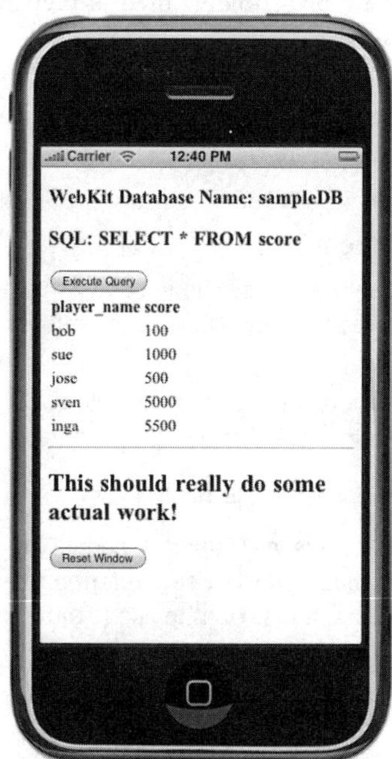

Figure 7.2 The browserAccessExample application after the Execute Query button is touched

Inserting data into the table is handled much the same way. If a record for an individual called Jane is inserted, the setData call is used, as seen in the following:

```
sampleDatabase.setData("INSERT INTO score VALUES('Jane', 250)");
```

It is unusual to hardcode values into SQL statements. Usually the values are due to user input. Although it is possible to build a SQL statement like the previous one from the information provided by the user, it can be dangerous to do so. The code that follows shows how to avoid this danger by using prepared statements.

```
function setScoresBCF(parameters){
   var name = document.getElementById('nameField').value;
   var score = document.getElementById('scoreField').value;
   var statementParameters = [name, score];
   var SQL = "INSERT INTO score VALUES(?, ?)";
  sampleDatabase.setData(SQL, statementParameters);
}
```

Notice that it looks different than the `setData` call used to create the `score` table. In the portion of the SQL string where a name and a score would be expected, question marks are found instead. These are placeholders used in prepared statements to indicate where the data in the `statementParameters` array should be inserted. It is the responsibility of the programmer to place the values to be inserted into the array in the order that they would have been placed in the SQL string. This is why the `name` variable is added to the `statementParameters` array before the `score` variable.

What Is a Prepared Statement?

Prepared statements dramatically increase the security of using SQL to store user-entered data. In fact, they are a good way to stop SQL injection attacks and should be used much more than they are.

Suppose you wanted to insert a record into a table called user_preferences with a location, color, and a song field. You could piece this together like this:

```
"SELECT * FROM user_preferences WHERE name = "+aName
```

Putting together SQL statements this way is bad. It cannot be emphasized enough how bad this is. It opens the entire database up to what is referred to as SQL insertion attacks. These are used to penetrate databases. Don't piece together SQL statements.

The safe way to do this is to create a SQL string that looks like this:

```
"SELECT * FROM user_preferences WHERE name = ?)"
```

Also create an array containing the value or values you want to use in place of question marks. The calls to setData and getData take care of the rest because they use a prepared statement.

In essence, when a prepared statement is used, the SQL is parsed before the question marks are replaced with the values. This means that if evil SQL is inserted into any of the variables, it is not parsed; to the database, it seems as if the SQL statement contains a strange string. A call such as the previous one using question marks would return no results. The pieced together one, on the other hand, can easily return everything from any table a hacker wants to see.

Prepared statements protect databases from intrusions known as SQL insertion attacks. Although it may seem silly to protect this small database from intrusion, it is not. There is always a way for someone who should not get access to a device or to the code running on the device to do damage. All computing should be done in a safe manner.

Removing data from a database is done in much the same way. Because the database is being modified, the `setData` method is used. Because the user supplies a name to be removed, a prepared statement is used for security reasons.

```
function deleteScoreBCF(parameters){
   var name = document.getElementById('nameField').value;
   var statementParameters = [blogName];
   database.setData('DELETE FROM score where name = ?',
                              statementParameters);
}
```

Section 3: Using Native SQLite Databases

In addition to being able to create and use databases in the WebKit engine found in every hybrid iPhone application, native databases can also be used. These databases enable creators of applications to include existing data in the installed application. For example, you might want to include a series of standard GPS locations in an application designed to help users find items in a retail market. Instead of downloading and storing the data when the application starts, you can include a SQLite database file in your application's installation.

The nativeDBAccess example application is identical in function to the browser DBAccess example, but it uses a SQLite database file called sample.sqlite. Figure 7.3 shows this file included in the Xcode project's Resources group.

The JavaScript code required to create a DataAccessObject that wraps the calls to a native database is different than what is used for the WebKit engine-based databases seen in Section 2. Just like with the WebKit database, the defining is done in the databaseDefinition.js file. However, in the case of native databases, only the name of the database file is needed. The version and size parameters are extraneous because native databases are unlimited in size (within reason), and versioning is part of the build and distribution process of the application's owner.

```
var sampleDatabase = sampleDatabase = new DataAccessObject("sample.sqlite");
```

Notice that there is no call to create a table because the score table already exists in the `sample.sqlite` file. It is possible to create tables in native databases, but it is unusual. The tables are usually added to the database file before the application is placed in Apple's App store.

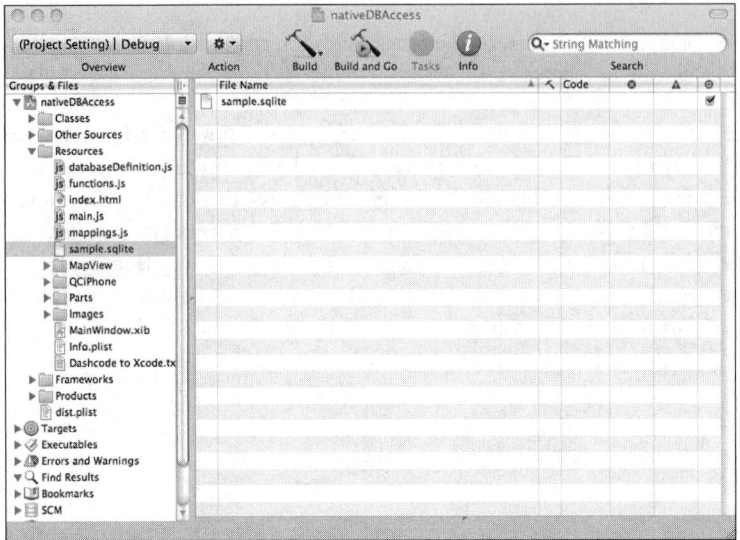

Figure 7.3 The resources of the nativeDBAccess example application

Retrieving data from a native database is almost exactly the same as getting it from a WebKit engine-managed database. The only difference, as shown in the following code, is that instead of using the `getData` method, the `getNativeData` method is used. From the application creator's point of view, the behaviors of these two methods are identical.

```
function getScoresBCF(parameters){
    debug('getting scores from database');
      var SQL = 'SELECT * FROM score';
    sampleDatabase.getNativeData(SQL);
}
```

The `getNativeData` method, just like the `getData` method discussed in Section 2, is asynchronous. Thus, the framework passes the collected data to other control objects mapped to the same command as the BCF when the data becomes available. As with the WebKit engine-managed example, this is the `displayScoresVCF` View Control Function.

Figure 7.4 shows the display generated by this VCF in the nativeDBAccess example application.

Adding and removing data and modifying the database is done in exactly the same way as seen in Section 2, with the exception that the setNativeData method is used instead of the setData method. As the creator of your application, the differences in behavior should be transparent to you.

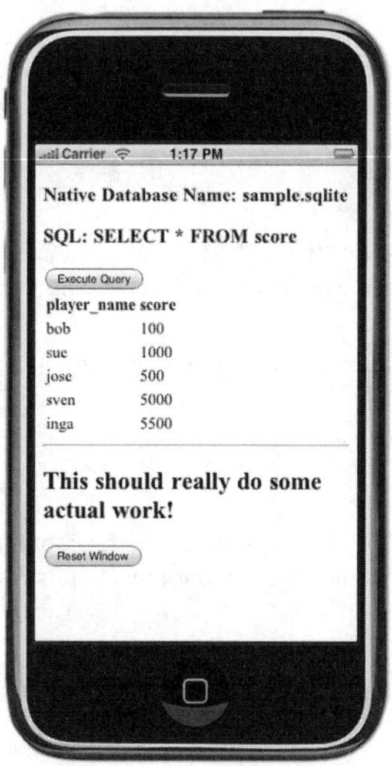

Figure 7.4 The nativeDBAccess example application after the Execute Query button is touched

Section 4: Using the DataAccessObject with WebKit Engine Databases

The previous sections covered how you can use the DataAccessObject to avoid having to know all of the intricacies of the SQLite WebKit engine and native implementations. This section shows you what those intricacies are and how to use them. If you just want to use the DataAccessObject and have no desire to know how it works, you can skip this section.

The purpose of the DataAccessObject found in the QCiPhone/DataAccessObject.js file is to require as little knowledge of SQLite from the programmer or engineer as possible. To this end, it has been engineered so that its methods and constructors are as much like the ServerAccessObject AJAX wrapper covered in Chapter 8, "Remote Data Access," as possible. By simplifying the API, it enables programmers who are not familiar with SQLite to store data without a steep learning curve.

The constructor for the DataAccessObject is the simplest of all its methods. The behavior is to set and define the object's methods as anonymous functions. This means that no attributes are needed to store the parameters passed into the constructor.

Anonymous Functions

When someone is anonymous, it means that you don't know what her name is. When a function is anonymous, it means it doesn't have a name. In JavaScript, a standard function has a name for it declared in a line such as

```
function bark(){}
```

In this case, the name of the function is bark. When a function needs to be passed to another function, it is common to use functions that have no names declared. These are called anonymous functions.

If an anonymous function is passed to bark, it looks something like this:

```
bark(new function(){
    //do something here
});
```

Notice that the scope operators for the anonymous function, {}, are contained in the parameter operators for the bark function, (). The bark function is now free to call or store this function as it desires.

All anonymous functions have access to local variables that could have been passed to the function in which they were declared. Because of this, the following code is valid:

```
String type = 'doberman';
bark(new function(){
    if(type == 'boxer'){
    }
    else if(type == 'doberman'){
    }
    .
    .
    .
});
```

This feature comes in handy when functions or methods have functions as parameters, as seen later in this section.

As with any powerful tool, it is important not to overuse anonymous functions when they are not needed.

As seen in Table 7.1 and discussed in Sections 2 and 3, the DataAccessObject has two major groups of methods. One handles data that is stored or retrieved using a WebKit engine-based database, and the other group handles data transfer between your JavaScript application and an SQLite database file included in your distributed application. The WebKit-based methods use the most JavaScript and are covered first.

Both the `getData` and `setData` methods are façades. They do minimal computation and rely on a third method to do most of the heavy work. The only real computation done by either of these methods involves the assembly of the values stored in the `passThroughParameters` variable seen in the code that follows.

```
this.getData = function(SQL, preparedStatementParameters){
        var passThroughParameters =
                        generatePassThroughParameters();
        this.dbAccess(SQL, preparedStatementParameters,
                              false, passThroughParameters);
    }
```

Because the W3C standards body responsible for the HTML 5 specification requires all calls to the WebKit engine database functionality be asynchronous, some information about the current state of the application must be passed along with requests so it can be used later. The generatePassThroughParameters function found in QCUtilities.js gathers these values.

As shown in the following code, these include the current command for which command objects are being called, the number of BCOs already called, the parameters passed to all of the control functions, such as `globalParamArray`, and an array that contains any results already generated by calls to other BCFs, such as `globalBCFResults`.

```
function generatePassThroughParameters(){
    var passThroughParameters = new Array();
    passThroughParameters.push(window.curCmd);
    passThroughParameters.push(window.numFuncsCalled);
    passThroughParameters.push(globalParamArray);
    passThroughParameters.push(window.globalBCFResults);
    return passThroughParameters;
}
```

These values are later used by the framework to ensure that any remaining control functions, based on the mappings defined in mappings.js for the `curCmd` command, are executed as if all command function calls were synchronous. See Chapter 2 for a further explanation of how this is accomplished.

The resultant `passThroughParameters` array is passed to the `dbAccess` method along with a flag indicating if the sql in the `SQL` variable should be treated as an attempt to change the data in the database. In the `getData` method, false is passed, as seen earlier.

The dbAccess method is the heart and soul of the DataAccessObject for WebKit engine databases. It does all the work when `getData` or `setData` are called.

To understand the `dbAccess` method, the underlying JavaScript SQLite API must first be understood. This API is included in the upcoming HTML 5 standard and is implemented in the WebKit engine use in the UIWebView found in all hybrid iPhone applications and in Mobile Safari. The most current version of this standard at the time of this writing can be found at http://www.w3.org/html/wg/html5/#sql. This standards document describes several objects and methods of objects, as shown in the following tables.

The basic item of this API is the Database object. Table 7.2 describes a function related to this object and one of its methods. The *`openDatabase`* function is a factory function that instantiates a Database object for you.

Table 7.2 **Database Object API**

Attribute/Method	Return	Description	Parameters
openDatabase (dbName, dbVersion, dbDescription, dbSize)	Database object	A factory function that creates a Database object for later use.	dbName—A uniquely identifying string used to reference the specific database. dbVersion—A string, usually in the form of a floating-point number. dbDescription—A string stating the purpose of the database. dbSize—The maximum amount of disk space allocated to the database in bytes. If null or nothing is passed, the default value of 5 megabytes is used.
transaction(executionCallback, errorCallback, successCallback)	SQLTransaction object	A method that creates a SQLTransaction object used to do database updates and queries.	executionCallback—A function containing the code required to execute the SQL. errorCallback—An optional function that is called if the transaction fails. Rollbacks of the database are not done in this method because rollback behavior is automatic in the case of failure. successCallback—An optional function called if the transaction is successful.

According to the standards document, all of `openDatabase`'s parameters are optional; however, it is unwise not to declare a database name. If you use multiple databases in various applications, each should have a distinct name. Leaving *`dbName`* blank can potentially cause only one database to be shared by all of your applications and can be easily available to nefarious applications written by others. To protect your databases, something similar to the *same origin rule* restricting AJAX calls in a browser is used.

The protection rule applied to databases is a restriction stating that a database can be accessed only by applications coming from the same origin. If you use databases in a web application served up from www.yourplace.com and another from web.yourplace.com, databases used in the different web applications would be accessible by both. In other words, anything served up from any yourspace.com origin can access all databases served up from that origin regardless of whether the database is created by the running application or one created by an application created by another subdomain in yourplace.com.

In hybrid applications, you use the UIWebView object instead of a web browser, and therefore, there is no *same origin rule* limiting AJAX. It is unknown at this time, but it can be assumed that the origin restriction for databases is not effective either. Because of this, the only thing protecting your database from being accessed by other applications might be that the writers of the other application don't know your database's name and version. Make sure you give your database a name and a version.

The *transaction* method is used by all SQL calls. In fact, there is no way to execute SQL against WebKit engine databases without using a *SQLTransaction* object created by the *transaction* method. Because of this, all JavaScript database calls in iPhone hybrid applications are automatically transaction-safe.

One item that usually concerns developers is when to roll back the database. This is usually done when the code written by a programmer detects that a transaction has failed in some manner. You don't need to worry about rollbacks when using the JavaScript database functionality because transactions handle their own rollbacks on failure.

Do not send a *ROLLBACK* SQL statement if your transaction fails. It has already been taken care of and causes trouble. The *errorCallBack* function passed to the transaction method is not used for this purpose. It is used only for notification of failures.

The *SQLTransaction* object has only one method, *executeSQL* (see Table 7.3). This method accepts any SQL you choose to send it. It is unwise to piece together a SQL statement and then execute it. You should use the builtin prepared statement functionality instead. If you are unsure what a prepared statement is and how to create one, look at Section 2.

Table 7.3 **The SQLTransaction Object API**

Attribute/Method	Return	Description	Parameters
executeSQL(sqlStatement, arguments, successCallback, errorCallback);	void	A method to execute any arbitrary SQL statement string.	sqlStatement—A string containing a valid SQL statement. It can have ? (question mark) place holders if it is to be treated as a prepared statement. Arguments—An optional array of values used to replace ? (question mark) place holders in prepared statements. successCallback—An optional function called upon successful execution of the sqlSatement. errorCallback—An optional function called if the execution of the sqlStatement fails.

In addition to the SQL statement, an optional parameter called arguments is passed in. This is an array of strings used to replace any question marks included in the SQL statement. These are used as the variables in the prepared statement created by the call to *executeSQL*. All calls to *executeSQL* create a prepared statement even if there are no place holders. This is safe if you use it. It also means that it is no faster if you do not.

The last two parameters are callback functions that are executed if the statement, not the transaction, succeeds or fails. The success function is passed a SQLResultSet object by the `executeSQL` method. The SQLResultSet API can be seen in Table 7.4. The failure function is passed a SQLError object. (The API for it can be seen in Table 7.6.) To handle the result of your execution of the SQL statement, you should implement these functions and include them in the `executeSQL` method call.

Table 7.4 **The SQLResultSet Object API**

Attribute/Method	Return	Description	Parameters
insertID	None	A read-only integer attribute containing the ID of a record inserted if the ID field is autoincrementing.	None
rowsAffected	None	A read-only integer attribute containing the number of rows added or changed during an update type statement.	None
rows	None	A SQLResultSetRowList attribute containing all of the resultant rows from a query type statement.	None

The SQLResultSet object contains the information you requested via the SQL statement. It also includes two items that are nice to have. These are the *insertID* and *rowsAffected* attributes.

If a table has an autoincrementing primary key and you insert a record into that table, the *insertID* attribute of the SQLResultSet will contain the autogenerated key value. This is handy when this key is needed to insert data associated with the key value into other tables.

After the successful execution of an insert or update SQL statement, the *rowsAffected* attribute contains the number of rows that was inserted or changed. This can be used to validate the behavior of complex SQL statements.

The third attribute of the SQLResultSet is the *rows* attribute. This attribute contains a SQLResultSetRowList, which is a wrapper around an array of records. As seen in Table 7.5, it has the attribute *length* that contains a number representing the number of records in the result of a SELECT type statement. This number matches the number of rows in the embedded array.

Table 7.5 **The SQLResultSetRowList Object API**

Attribute/Method	Return	Description	Parameters
length	None	A read-only attribute containing the number of records fetched by a query type statement.	None
item(index)	Array	A method that returns a record as a JavaScript associative array or map.	Index—the result set record number to be returned.

It also has a method that is used to access individual rows of the results called `item`. This method and attribute make it easy to iterate over the rows and values in the rows using embedded `for` loops. The standard methodology for doing such iterations looks like the code that follows.

```
1 for( var i = 0; i < aResultSet.length; i++){
2     var aRow = aResultSet.item(i);
3     for(key in aRow){
4         var aValue = aRow[key];
5         //do something with the key and the value
6     }
7 }
```

Although the for loop code above is what many would consider a standard methodology, it is not optimal in its execution because, in line 1, the length of the result set is retrieved each time the code goes through the outer loop. Another point of waste is the repeated use of the for-each loop in line 3.

JavaScript for-each loops are particularly wasteful with respect to CPU cycles, but are particularly bad when they are used in other loops. Later in this section, the explanation of the `dbAccess` method shows how this code can be changed to be more optimal in its execution.

If there is any sort of error in executing the SQL statement—whether it be because of a statement failure, a SQLError object is generated instead of the SQLResultSet object. Just as a SQLResultSet is passed to the success function used as a parameter to the statement's `executeSQL` method, a SQLError is passed to the failure function.

Your success function is never passed an SQLError nor is your error function ever passed a SQLResultSet. This enables each of these functions to have a single purpose, and therefore, these functions become easier to create, write, and maintain.

The SQLError object contains two attributes that contain an error code number and an error message generated by SQLite (see Table 7.6).

Table 7.6 **The SQLError Object API**

Attribute/Method	Return	Description	Parameters
code	None	A read-only attribute containing the error number code. The possible codes are: 0—Transaction failed for unknown reason. 1—Statement failed for unknown reason. 2—Statement failed because the expected version of the database isn't the actual version of the database. 3—Statement failed because too much data was returned. Try using the SQL "LIMIT" modifier. 4—Statement failed because the memory limit was reached and the user didn't okay increasing the memory limit. 5—The statement failed because of a locking failure in the transaction. 6—an INSERT, UPDATE, or REPLACE statement failed because it violated a constraint such as duplicating a unique key.	None
message	None	A read-only attribute containing an appropriate error message.	None

These two items, `code` and `message`, are useful to a programmer or engineer, but should not be displayed to a user. They will not know what they mean. Use these indicators to log the error and to display something helpful to the user.

Examples of how to use each of these objects are in the `dbAccess` method of the DataAccessObject. As mentioned earlier in this section, the `dbAccess` method has five parameters and is the worker method behind the `getData` and `setData` façade methods. Its fourth parameter indicates whether the access being requested is to modify the database or to query it. This parameter is set by the façade function calling `dbAccess`.

When examining the `dbAccess` method, you will find that it uses several anonymous functions. The first of these is passed as the first and only parameter to the database's `transaction` method on line 3. It might appear to be easier to define this as a regular function elsewhere in the code and pass it as the first parameter. However, this makes the remaining code difficult, if not impossible, because variables that are in scope because they use anonymous functions are no longer in scope. Line 2 in the following code instantiates the QueryResult object that is used as the return value of the `dbAccess` method.

For a QueryResult object to be of real use, it must be available inside the transaction's `executeSql` function. Other than using anonymous functions, the only way to make this QueryResult object available in that underlying function is to make it global.

If it was global in scope, there could be only one database access at a time. Because all database access is asynchronous, this is impossible to guarantee. Therefore, the best approach to take is to use anonymous functions. This same logic also applies to the functions passed to the `executeSql` method of the transaction itself.

The `executeSql` method of the Transaction object can be passed two functions as parameters. It is a best practice to always do so. The second parameter, as shown in Table 7.6, is intended to be the function that handles the results of your query if all goes well. This function declaration begins on line 10 in the code that follows.

In the success function, any inserted ID generated by the SQL is stored in the QueryResult instantiated on line 7. If rows in the database are changed, the number of the rows affected is also set. This is done only if the `treatAsChangeData` parameter of the `dbAccess` method is set to true.

If data is not changed, a query must have been executed. Lines 23–51 handle this condition. In these code lines, a two-dimensional JavaScript array is created that is attached to the QueryResult return value and stores all of the data found in the SQLResult set. By transferring the data to a standard JavaScript array, you can access the data in your other code without knowing the structure of the SQLResult object or the fields returned from the query. If you do want to know the field names, they are also stored in the QueryResult object for later use. The field names and the field values retain the order in which they are found in the SQLResult.

```
1 this.dbAccess = function(SQL, preparedStatementParameters,
2                   treatAsChangeData, passThroughParameters){
3    if(!this.db){
4        this.db = openDatabase(dbName, dbVersion,
5                              dbDescription, dbSize);
6    }
7    var queryResult = new QueryResult();
8    this.db.transaction(function(tx) {
9          tx.executeSql(SQL, preparedStatementParameters,
10       function(tx, resultSet) {
11                 if(treatAsChangeData){
12                    try{
13               queryResult.insertedID = resultSet.insertId;
14               queryResult.rowsAffected =
15                          resultSet.rowsAffected;
16             }
17             catch(ex){
18               //then must have been an update
19               queryResult.rowsAffected =
20                          resultSet.rowsAffected;
21             }
22          }
23          else{
24              //not a change to the database.
```

```
            //must be a query
            queryResult.numRowsFetched =
                        resultSet.rows.length;
            var dataArray = new Array();
            queryResult.numResultFields = 0;
            queryResult.fieldNames = new Array();
            if(queryResult.numRowsFetched > 0){
                //retrieve the field ids in the result set
                firstRecord = resultSet.rows.item(0);
                var numFields = 0;
                for(key in firstRecord){
                     queryResult.fieldNames.push(key);
                     numFields++;
                }
                queryResult.numResultFields = numFields;
                var numRecords =
                        queryResult.numRowsFetched;
                for(var i = 0; i < numRecords; i++){
                   var record = resultSet.rows.item(i);
                   var row = new Array();
                   dataArray.push(row);
                   for(var j = 0; j < numFields; j++){
                   row.push(
                      record[queryResult.fieldNames[j]]);
                }
            }
        }
        queryResult.data = dataArray;
     }
     if(window.callFunc){
        var theResults = new Array();
        theResults.push(queryResult);
        theResults.push(passThroughParameters);
        requestHandler(passThroughParameters[0],
                       passThroughParameters[2], theResults);
    }
}//end of sql execute success callback function
, function(tx, error) {
      queryResult.errorMessage =  error.message;
      if(window.callFunc){
         var theResults = new Array();
         theResults.push(queryResult);
         theResults.push(passThroughParameters);
         requestHandler(passThroughParameters[0],
                        passThroughParameters[2], theResults);
   }
```

```
71  }//end of main sql execute fail callback function
72  );//end of main executeSql call
73  });//end of transaction callback function
74 }//end of dbAccess method
```

Regardless of whether the SQL statement that is executed is a database change or a query, the QueryResult object created at the beginning of the function call is dispatched to any and all remaining, uncalled control functions by the framework. This is done on lines 58 and 59 using the `requestHandler` function discussed in Chapter 2.

Line 62 is the beginning of the error-handling function declaration for the Transaction object method. Its responsibility is to insert the error message generated by SQLite into the QueryResult and then dispatch this to your remaining control functions. For more information on control functions, see Chapter 2.

Section 5: Using the DataAccessObject with Native Databases

Less JavaScript code is required to access native databases than what is required to access WebKit engine databases. Most of the work is done on the Objective-C side of the framework.

As with the `getData` and `setData` methods described in the previous section, the `getNativeData` and `setNativeData` methods are façades. In this case, they do not call the `dbAccess` method of the DataAccessObject but call the `getDeviceData` function found in the QCUtilities.js file.

```
this.getNativeData =
     function(SQL, preparedStatementParameters){
          getDeviceData(dbName, SQL,
         preparedStatementParameters);
}
this.setNativeData =
     function(SQL, preparedStatementParameters){
          setDeviceData(dbName, SQL,
          preparedStatementParameters);
}
```

The `getDeviceData` function has two major pieces of functionality. The first, shown in lines 4–16, is to put together an array of information needed to execute the query in Objective-C. Included with this array are the pass-through parameters, discussed in the previous section. These pass-through parameters are required because, as in dealing with the WebKit engine database requests, this request is asynchronous. For more information on asynchronous computing, see Chapter 2.

The array being created contains the database name, the SQL to be executed, any prepared statement parameters required by the SQL, and the pass-through parameters. Information regarding prepared statements is found in the previous section of this chapter.

```
function getDeviceData(dbName, SQL,
            preparedStatementParameters, callBackParams){
      if(dbName && SQL){
            var dataArray = new Array();
            dataArray.push(dbName);
            dataArray.push(SQL);
            if(preparedStatementParameters){
                  dataArray.push(preparedStatementParameters);
            }
            else{
                  //put in a placeholder
                  dataArray.push(new Array());
            }
            var callBackParameters =
                 generatePassThroughParameters();
            dataArray.push(callBackParameters);

            var dataString = JSON.stringify(dataArray);
            makeCall("getData", dataString);
      }
     return null;
}
```

After the data is prepared, it is turned into a JSON string and passed to the `makeCall` function. This `makeCall` function triggers the Objective-C side of the framework as seen in Chapter 4, "GPS, Acceleration, and Other Native Functions with QuickConnect." This is the second major piece of functionality. Without it, native databases would not be accessible. For more information on JSON, see Appendix A, "Introduction to JSON."

Like the functions in Chapter 4 that access native data, Objective-C control objects are needed to handle the actual retrieval of the database data. The two objects—SetDataBCO and GetDataBCO—interact with the database whether the database is modified or queried. This is like the `getData` and `setData` JavaScript functions.

```
+ (id) doCommand:(NSArray*) parameters{
    if( [parameters count] >= 3){
        NSString *dbName = [parameters objectAtIndex:1];
        NSString *SQL = [parameters objectAtIndex:2];
        NSArray *perparedStatementValues = nil;
        if([parameters count] == 4){
            perparedStatementValues = [parameters
                                objectAtIndex:3];
        }
            SQLiteDataAccess *aDBAccess = [SQLiteDataAccess
                  getInstance:dbName isWriteable:YES];
            return [aDBAccess getData:SQL
                  withParameters:perparedStatementValues];
    }
    return nil;
```

```
}
@end
```

Also, like the JavaScript `get` and `setData` functions, these BCOs do little actual computation. In the previous code, the `doCommand` method retrieves the database name, the SQL, and any prepared statement parameters passed from the JavaScript request.

After these pieces of information are available, a call to the SQLiteDataAccess object's `getData` method is made. This object is essentially a mirror of the JavaScript DataAccessObject. It has `getData` and `setData` methods, but unlike the JavaScript version, the Objective-C version is a singleton. If you need more information regarding singletons, see Chapter 4.

The SQLiteDataAccess `getData` and `setData` methods, like their JavaScript counterparts, are façades of a `dbAccess` method. Like the JavaScript `dbAccess` method, the Objective-C version is particularly complex. This is because of the complexity of the SQLite API for the libsqlite3.0.dylib dynamic library that ships on every iPhone and iPod touch, as shown in Table 7.7.

Table 7.7 **The SQLite3 API**

Object/Function	Return	Description	Parameters
sqlite3	None	An object representing the SQLite database in memory.	None
sqlite3_open (filePath, &aDatabase)	SQLITE_ OK if successfully opened	Opens the database file located at filePath and stores the pointer in the aDatabase pointer.	filePath—The full path on the machine to the SQLite data file. aDatabase—A pointer reference to a SQLite3 pointer that represents the in-memory database.
sqlite3_close (aDatabase)	void	Closes the connections to the SQLite database file.	ADatabase—A SQLite3 pointer set in the sqlite3_open function.
sqlite3_errmsg (aDatabase)	const char *	Retrieves the last error generated.	ADatabase—A SQLite3 pointer to the database from which an error message is desired.
sqlite3_stmt	None	A single SQL prepared statement.	None

Table 7.7 **The SQLite3 API**

Object/Function	Return	Description	Parameters
sqlite3_prepare_v2 (aDatabase, SQLChar, -1, &statement, NULL)	int SQLite_ OK on success	Interprets the SQL.	aDatabase—A SQLite3 pointer to the database SQLChar—Const char * of UTF8 characters that are the SQL string.
sqlite3_column_ count(statement)	int	Counts the number of fields in the result set of a query.	Statement—A SQLite3_stmt pointer.
sqlite3_column_name (statement, i)	const char *	Gets the field name for a field.	Statement—A sqlite3_stmt pointer. I—An integer representing the field number
sqlite3_changes(data base)	int	Retrieves the number of records affected by a change to a table.	aDatabase—A SQLite3 pointer to the database.
sqlite3_step(stateme nt)	int SQLITE_ROW when a row is available	Moves the caret in the result set to the next record.	statement—A sqlite3_stmt pointer.
sqlite3_column_type(statement,i)	int Possible values: SQLITE_INTEGER SQLITE_FLOAT SQLITE_BLOB SQLITE_NULL SQLITE_TEXT	Gets the type of a field (column) in a result set for a statement.	statement—A sqlite3_stmt pointer. i—The number of the field for which the data is desired.
sqlite3_column_int(st atement, i)	int	Gets the value out of an integer type field.	statement—A sqlite3_stmt pointer. i—The number of the field for which the data is desired.
sqlite3_column_doubl e(statement, i)	double	Gets the value out of a double type field.	Statement—A SQLite3_stmt pointer. i—The number of the field for which the data is desired.

Table 7.7 **The SQLite3 API**

Object/Function	Return	Description	Parameters
sqlite3_column_text(statement, i)	const unsigned char *	Gets the value out of a string type field.	statement—A SQLite3_stmt pointer. i—The number of the field for which the data is desired.
sqlite3_column_blob(statement, i)	byte *	Gets the bytes out of a binary large object (BLOB) type field.	statement—A SWLite3_stmt pointer. i—The number of the field for which the data is desired.
sqlite3_column_bytes(statement,i)	int	Gets the number of bytes in a value in a BLOB type field.	statement—A SQLite3_stmt pointer. i—The number of the field for which the data is desired.
sqlite3_finalize(statement)	void	Releases the resources associated with the statement.	statement—A sqlite3_stmt pointer.
sqlite3_bind_blob(statement, parameterIndex, aVariable, byteLength, transienceKey)	int	Binds a pointer to a byte array to a prepared statement place holder.	statement—A SQLite3_stmt pointer. parameterIndex—The index number of the prepared statement place holder. aVariable—A pointer to the byte array to be stored in the database. byteLength—The number of bytes to store. TransienceKey—An indicator for if the data being inserted should be copied prior to insertion to keep the data from changing during storage.

Table 7.7 **The SQLite3 API**

Object/Function	Return	Description	Parameters
sqlite3_bind_double(statement, parameterIndex, aVariable)	int	Binds a double to a prepared statement place holder.	Statement—A SQLite3_stmt pointer. parameterIndex—The index number of the prepared statement place holder. aVariable—A double to be stored in the database.
sqlite3_bind_int(statement, parameterIndex, aVariable)	int	Binds an integer to a prepared statement place holder.	Statement—A SQLite3_stmt pointer. parameterIndex—The index number of the prepared statement place holder. aVariable—An integer to be stored in the database.

This C library contains all of the functions used to access SQLite databases and includes capabilities such as transactions and prepared statements. The code that follows shows how to use the API to do prepared statements. It is found in the dbAccess method of the SQLiteDataAccess object. As stated in the API, the `sqlite3_prepare_v2` function must be passed pointers to the database, the SQL to execute, as well as a pointer pointer to a `sqlite3_stmt` variable. If an error happens during the execution of the SQL, `sqlite3_prepare_v2` returns a numeric error code.

```
int numResultColumns = 0;
sqlite3_stmt *statement = nil;
const char* SQLChar = [SQL UTF8String];
if (sqlite3_prepare_v2(database, SQLChar, -1,
            &statement, NULL) == SQLITE_OK) {
      .
      .
      .
}
```

The `sqlite3_stmt` variable passed in the previous code is set during the execution of the `sqlite3_prepare_v2` function and contains the `sqlite3_stmt` that is then used to retrieve the individual data elements in the result set of an executed SQL query. Multiple calls to the `sqlite3_step` function move a caret that keeps track of the row position in the result set. Thus, if the result set is empty, or contains no rows, `sqlite3_step` does not return `SQLITE_ROW` but returns `SQLITE_DONE` instead. This enables you to use a `while` statement to retrieve the data out of the row the caret points to.

```
while (sqlite3_step(statement) == SQLITE_ROW) {
    .
    .
    .
}
```

In this while loop, a series of NSMutableArrays is created as seen on line 218 of the SQLiteDataAccess.m file and in the line that follows. Each of these arrays represents a row of results that are retrieved and therefore called `row`.

```
NSMutableArray *row = [[NSMutableArray alloc]
    initWithCapacity:numResultColumns];
```

To get the individual values out of the fields for each of the result set's records, calls must be made to get the data as the correct type. Table 7.7 lists the functions available for getting these different types, and the code that follows shows each of these being called.

```
int type  = [[[theResult columnTypes]
      objectAtIndex:i] intValue];
if(type == SQLITE_INTEGER){
    NSNumber *aNum = [[NSNumber alloc]
            initWithInt: sqlite3_column_int(statement, i)];
     [row addObject:aNum];
     [aNum autorelease];
}
else if(type == SQLITE_FLOAT){
NSNumber *aFloat = [[NSNumber alloc]
      initWithFloat
            :sqlite3_column_double(statement, i)];
     [row addObject:aFloat];
     [aFloat autorelease];
}
else if(type == SQLITE_TEXT){
NSString *aText = [[NSString alloc]
      initWithCString:sqlite3_column_text(statement, i)
      encoding:NSASCIIStringEncoding];
     [row addObject:aText];
     [aText autorelease];
}
else if(type == SQLITE_BLOB){
NSData *aData = [[NSData alloc]
      dataWithBytes:sqlite3_column_blob(statement, i)
            length:sqlite3_column_bytes(statement,i)];
     [row addObject:aData];
     [aData autorelease];
```

```
}
else{//SQLITE_NULL
      [row addObject:@"null"];
}
```

To make calls to the correct function, the type of the field in question must have already been determined. To facilitate this, the field types are discovered and stored prior to making these calls, as seen in lines 199–205 in the SQLiteDataAccess.m file and in the code that follows.

```
NSMutableArray *columnTypes = [[NSMutableArray alloc]
                        initWithCapacity:0];
for(int i = 0; i < numResultColumns; i++){
      NSNumber * columnType = [NSNumber numberWithInt:
      sqlite3_column_type(statement,i)];
      [columnTypes addObject:columnType];
}
[theResult setColumnTypes:columnTypes];
```

The type of individual columns is retrieved from the statement's result set using the `sqlite3_column_type` function. Pass the statement pointer and the number of the field for which the type is desired to the function, and it returns a numeric indicator of the type of that field. The possible types are:

- SQLITE_INTEGER
- SQLITE_FLOAT
- SQLITE_BLOB
- SQLITE_NULL
- SQLITE_TEXT

The return type of the `dbAccess`, `setData`, and `getData` methods is a DataAccessResult pointer. This object contains the results of the execution of any SQL string against a SQLite database. The following code is from the DataAccessResult.h file and shows the fields used to store the results of one SQL execution.

```
@interface DataAccessResult : NSObject {
    NSArray *fieldNames;
    NSArray *columnTypes;
    NSArray *results;
    NSString *errorDescription;
     NSInteger rowsAffected;
     NSInteger insertedID;
}
@property (nonatomic, retain) NSArray *fieldNames;
@property (nonatomic, retain) NSArray *columnTypes;
@property (nonatomic, retain) NSArray *results;
@property (nonatomic, retain) NSString *errorDescription;
```

```
@property (nonatomic) NSInteger rowsAffected;
@property (nonatomic) NSInteger insertedID;

- (NSString*) JSONStringify;

@end
```

As discussed in Chapter 4, because the framework handles data passing all DataAccess-Result objects generated by calls to the SQLiteDataAccess object are included in the parameters sent to your View Control Objects (VCO). Because a call is being made from JavaScript to get or set data in a "native" database, the end results of the query must be passed back to the JavaScript application. This is done by the SendDBResultVCO object.

As with all command objects, SendDBResultVCO has a `doCommand` method. Because of the need to transfer the data back to JavaScript, the results are converted into a JSON string. Lines 8–11 of the following code show how this is done. Each result is first turned into a JSON string and added to the NSMutableArray `retVal`. The `retVal` array is then converted into a JSON string. Because of limitations in the Objective-C JSON library, it is not possible to have arrays of objects and make one JSON string creation call. The JSON library doesn't traverse down through objects in arrays to make accurate conversions. Thus, the extra call to `JSONStringify` is needed for each DataAccessResult object.

```
1 + (id) doCommand:(NSArray*) parameters{
      .
      .
      .
2     NSArray *results = [parameters subarrayWithRange:aRange];
3     int numResults = [results count];
4     NSMutableArray *retVal = [[NSMutableArray alloc] init];
5     for(int i = 0; i < numResults; i++){
6         DataAccessResult * aResult =
7                (DataAccessResult*)[results objectAtIndex:i];
8         NSString* resultString = [aResult JSONStringify];
9         [retVal addObject:resultString];
10    }
11    [retVal addObject:[parameters objectAtIndex:4]];
12
13    SBJSON *generator = [SBJSON alloc];
14    NSError *error;
15    NSString *dataString = [generator stringWithObject:retVal error:&error];
16    [generator release];
17    dataString = [dataString
18                stringByReplacingOccurrencesOfString:@"'" withString:@"\\'"];
19    NSString *jsString = [[NSString alloc]
20            initWithFormat:
21                @"handleRequestCompletionFromNative('%@')
```

```
                          , dataString];
   QuickConnectViewController *controller =
                 [parameters objectAtIndex:0];
    [controller.webView
          stringByEvaluatingJavaScriptFromString:jsString]);
     return nil;
}
```

Just as in Chapter 4, where the results are converted into a JSON string, a call is made that passes them to the JavaScript side of the application for further processing. This is the call to `stringByEvaluatingJavaScriptFromString` seen previously. It executes the `handleRequestCompletionFromNative` JavaScript function that ensures that the rest of the BCOs and VCOs map to the original command. See Chapter 5, "Hybrid Applications, GPS, Acceleration, and Other Native Functions with PhoneGap," for how this is done.

Summary

The DataAccesObject JavaScript module makes it significantly easier to interact with SQLite databases in the WebKit engine. Because the module accepts only standard JavaScript types, such as strings and arrays, it is easier to call than the WebKit engine's JavaScript SQLite functions themselves. The DataAcecessObject is also a façade that is used to access "native" database files you can ship with your application. By making JavaScript calls, you can access data in databases. This makes your JavaScript application a full-fledged application just as if you had written it in Objective-C.

Like the DataAccessObject in JavaScript, the Objective-C SQLiteDataAccess class makes it much easier to pull data out of or put data into SQLite databases that you ship with your application. It follows the same design as the JavaScript DataAccessObject so that if you don't know Objective-C, it is easier to learn and understand what it is doing.

Because all query results from the WebKit engine or to the "native" databases are objects that contain standard JavaScript types, you do not need to know about SQLite, WebKit-based, or "native" internals.

Both the DataAccessObject and the SQLiteDataAccess class give you transaction safety to keep asynchronous calls from disrupting your requests. You can safely make any number of concurrent database calls without worrying about disrupting the data in the database. The next chapter covers how to make a wrapper for AJAX calls that looks and behaves much like the DataAccessObject.

8

Remote Data Access

Sometimes, your application might need to access data from a remote database or from one or more web services. You might even want to synchronize the data on the phone with data stored remotely.

Hybrid iPhone applications make this easy. Because they are hybrids, they have full access to the XMLHttpRequest object in JavaScript. This chapter shows you how to retrieve data from an RSS feed and display it in your application.

As with the database access discussed in Chapter 7, "Database Access," an easy-to-use wrapper for the XMLHttpRequest object is explained in the first section. Later sections explain how the wrapper is created and its inner workings.

Section 1: BrowserAJAXAccess Example Application

In Chapter 7, the nativeDBAccess example application shows the storing and retrieving data process using an SQLite database on a device. This chapter uses a similar application to interact with web services and servers to retrieve data. You can find the browserAJAXAcces application folder in the Examples directory of the quickconnectiPhone folder you downloaded from *sourceforge.net/projects/quickconnect/*. Figure 8.1 shows this example application running.

All WordPress blogs have an RSS feed that serves up the latest ten blog entries of any hosted blog, as seen in Figure 8.2. Although it appears that this feed doesn't serve up full blog entries, it actually does. The browserAJAXAccess application shows only the headlines, but can easily be extended to store the headlines and the postings using the approach and code shown in Chapter 7.

Thankfully, all RSS feeds are client-agnostic; they don't care what the client is. A feed gets a request for blog postings and sends them out as XML regardless of who or what requests them. Because the UIWebView contains the WebKit engine, it can send requests to the feed and interpret the XML returned. The tool that is used to do this is the XMLHttpRequest object, and the methodology to accomplish this is called AJAX.

Figure 8.1 The browserAJAXAccess application showing the blog listing for TetonTech

AJAX Is Not Greek

One of the greatest written creations of all time is the *Iliad*. This epic poem by Homer is concerned with the war between the Greeks, also known as the Achaeans, and the Trojans.

One of the greatest heroes of the Greeks is AJAX. Repeatedly, he defeats his opponents, and in one instance, he single handedly saves the Greek fleet from destruction.

Just like the Greek fleet, traditional web page development has been and is under attack. It is viewed as too slow, too hard to use, and inflexible. Once again, an AJAX comes to the rescue, but this one is not Greek. This AJAX stands for Asynchronous JavaScript and XML.

The concept behind AJAX is simple. Give the user a richer experience by not reloading pages every time he makes a request. Instead, send or retrieve data and then use dynamic HTML principles to display the result. All of this can be done in one HTML page by using JavaScript.

AJAX should not be Greek to you.

By combining the XMLHttpRequest object with some simple JavaScript to manipulate a web page, your hybrid iPhone application can use remote data just as if it were local data. You then get the best of both worlds: Your application can run in standalone mode,

Figure 8.2 The TetonTech RSS feed as seen in the Safari browser

run in networked mode, and can synchronize any data differences when a connection is available. The QuickConnectiPhone framework provides you with an easy-to-use AJAX wrapper, the ServerAccessObject.

Section 2: Using the ServerAccessObject

The ServerAccessObject AJAX wrapper enables you to easily access remote data without knowing the details of the XMLHttpRequest object's API. The ServerAccesObject API is nearly the same as the DataAccessObject discussed in Chapter 7.

Like its API, the API for the ServerAccessObject has one constructor and two methods. The constructor stores the URL of the remote server and sets up the object's methods. The two methods—`getData` and `setData`—can then retrieve data from and send data to the remote server defined in the constructor. Table 8.1 shows the ServerAccess Object's API.

Table 8.1 **The ServerAccessObject API**

Attribute/Method	Return	Description	Parameters
ServerAccessObject (URL)	Server Access Object	Creates a ServerAccessObject when called with the new key word.	URL—The URL for the server to be contacted.
getData (dataType, refresh, parameterSequence, HTTPHeaders)	void	A method used to retrieve information from a remote server. This is a GET type of request. This method is thread-safe.	dataType—The type of data being retrieved. It is one of two options: ServerAccessObject.XML or ServerAccessObject.TEXT. refresh—A Boolean indicating whether a forced refresh of the data from the server is to be performed. parameterSequence—Any parameters to be added to the URL. Do not include the initial ? (question mark) in this sequence. HTTPHeaders—An associative array of request header names and values to be sent with the request.
setData(dataType, parameterSequence, data, HTTPHeaders)	void	A method used to modify or create information on a remote server or to pass secure types of parameters. This is a POST type of request. This method is thread-safe.	dataType—The type of data being retrieved. It is one of two options: ServerAccessObject.XML or ServerAccessObject.TEXT. parameterSequence—Any parameters to be added to the URL. Do not include the initial ? (question mark) in this sequence. data—Any data you want to include in the send. This can be large amounts of character type information, file uploads, and so on. HTTPHeaders—An associative array of request header names and values to be sent with the request.

The ServerAccessObject.js file found in the QCiPhone group in both the Dashcode and Xcode templates contains the ServerAccessObject wrapper. This JavaScript file is automatically included in the index.html file of your application by both templates.

The `getSiteDataBCF` function uses this JavaScript class in the functions.js file. This JavaScript file contains all of the control functions for the browserAJAX example application. For more information on what these types of functions are and how to create them, see Chapter 2, "JavaScript Modularity and iPhone Applications."

The purpose of the `getSiteDataBCF` function is to retrieve the blog entries from the author's blog. Such retrievals are easily done using the ServerAccessObject, as shown in lines 2–5 in the following code.

```
1 function getSiteDataBCF(parameters){
2        var site = new ServerAccessObject(
3                        'http://tetontech.wordpress.com/feed/');
4     site.getData(ServerAccessObject.XML,
5                        ServerAccessObject.REFRESH);
6       //Since the  AJAX data access call is asynchronous
7   //this BCF should return nothing.
8
9 }
```

Lines 2 and 3 show the construction of the ServerAccessObject. It is passed the URL of the RSS feed to be consumed. In this case, the URL of the author's blog, http://TetonTech.wordpress.com/feed is used. To access another WordPress blog, replace this URL.

Lines 4 and 5 can then use this new object called `site` to get the data. Because this is an RSS feed and it is known that the server will send XML type data back to the iBlog application, the data type is set to XML. The second parameter is a flag that forces a refresh of the data instead of using a cached version. This is required if you want to ensure the data you receive contains any and all changes stored on the server.

Indiscriminate use of forcing a refresh can have adverse side effects. Forcing a refresh when it is not required can cause server and network overload if your application becomes popular. For this reason, you should evaluate whether the absolute latest data is required or whether it can be slightly out of date.

Just like the DataAccessObject, all calls to the ServerAccessObject are asynchronous. Several calls can be run at the same time as long as there is a new ServerAccessObject created for each call. If you use the QuickConnectiPhone framework, you do not need to define a callback function as you would when using AJAX. The framework ensures that any remaining Business Control Functions (BCF) and View Control Functions (VCF) mapped to the same command as the BCF making the ServerAccessObject calls are executed.

The `getSiteDataBCF` and `displaySiteDataVCF` functions are both mapped to the `sampleQuery` command in the mappings.js file as discussed in Chapter 2. This means that the data requested by `getSiteDataBCF` is guaranteed to be passed to `displaySiteDataVCF` by the framework.

The code for `displaySiteDataVCF` is found in the following code. The `results` parameter passed to this function is an array of JavaScript objects, one for each BCF mapped to the `sampleQuery` command. The `getData` method of the ServerAccessObject results in the creation of a QueryResult object just like the `getData` method of the DataAccess Object (see Chapter 7 for information about the QueryResult object).

After clearing displayed items represented by the `container` variable in the following code, the QueryResult object containing the results of the AJAX call is retrieved on line 9. Because `getSiteDataBCF` is the first BCF mapped to the `sampleQuery` command, the result generated by its call for data is the first object in the `results` array parameter.

As seen in Chapter 7, QueryResult objects have an attribute named `data`. In the case of XML requests such as the one in `getSiteDataBCF`, the data attribute is populated with the resulting XML document.

Because it is a document similar to the HTML document that is usually used in dynamic HTML, it is treated much the same. The same types of methods are available, such as `getElementById` and `getElementsByTagName`. It is also composed of `Node` objects in parent, child, and sibling relationships. You can use all of the standard methods and approaches to interpret the data.

The call to a helper function `parseWordPressFeed` found in the RSSUtilities.js file is also on line 9. It uses these standard methods to retrieve a two-dimensional array of blog postings called `entries`. Each entry found in the array is composed of the posting date, the posting content, and the posting title.

```
1 function displaySiteDataVCF(results, parameters){
2    var container =
3                    document.getElementById('queryResults');
4     //clear the contents of the container
5     while(container.lastChild){
6         container.removeChild(container.lastChild);
7     }
8     //use a wordpress parser to create entry objects
9     var entries = parseWordPressFeed(results[0].data);
10     var numEntries = entries.length;
11     //for each entry insert the title and date
12        //into the container div
13     for (var i = numEntries-1; i >= 0; i--){
14         var entry = entries[i];
15         var publishDate = entry.date;
16         var title = entry.title;
17
18         var titleElement = document.createElement('h2');
19         titleElement.innerText = entry.title;
20         container.appendChild(titleElement);
21
22         var dateElement = document.createElement('h3');
23         dateElement.innerText = entry.date;
24         container.appendChild(dateElement);
25
```

```
26         var hardRule = document.createElement('hr');
27         container.appendChild(hardRule);
28     }
29 }
```

As each entry generated by the parseWordPressFeed helper function is accessed, lines 13–28 create HTML Element objects and insert them into the container. This causes the display to contain the title and date of each blog entry. A hard rule is then added to separate each displayed entry.

This example shows how to handle RSS feeds, but other types of access are just as easy, if not easier. You can make a request of type TEXT and retrieve HTML to insert into your application's user interface, though this is discouraged for security reasons. You can also make a TEXT type call to retrieve JSON.

JSON Isn't Greek, Either

JSON is pronounced "Jason" as in Jason and the Argonauts. It is interesting that Jason and his companions were noted for their long voyage to retrieve the Golden Fleece.

JSON is how JavaScript objects can travel long distances across networks. It stands for JavaScript Object Notation. This is a fancy title for something that has been around for a long time.

The following code shows how to create a JavaScript object and store a first and last name in it:

```
var anObject = new Object();
anObject.fName = 'bob';
anObject.lName = 'jones';
```

Or, the following code shows how to use object notation:

```
var anObject = {fName:'bob', lName:'jones'};
```

Which is correct? Both accomplish the same thing. The second option is more than likely faster, but when objects get large, the first option is more readable and supportable.

The advantage of object notation is that it can be sent anywhere as a character string, such as:

```
"{fName:'bob', lName:'jones'}"
```

It can then turn into an object by passing it to the standard JavaScript function eval, but is dangerous to do this. For a safer and easy-to-use methodology, see Appendix A, "Introduction to JSON."

Is it a coincidence that two Greek heroes, AJAX and JSON, are saving web type development? This is left for you to decide.

Whatever the type of data you need to retrieve, the ServerAccessObject makes it easy. Simply instantiate the object and call `getData` for a GET type call or `setData` for a

POST type call. Either way, the QuickConnectiPhone framework passes the information to all subsequent control objects you have mapped to your command.

Section 3: ServerAccessObject

The previous section covered how you can use the ServerAccessObject to avoid having to know AJAX and the XMLHttpRequest API. This section shows you what these are and how to use them. If you just want to use the ServerAccessObject and have no desire to know how it works, you can skip this section.

The purpose of the ServerAccessObject, found in the QciPhone/ServerAccessObject.js file, is to require as little knowledge of AJAX from the programmer or engineer as possible. To this end, it is engineered so that its methods and constructors are similar to the DataAccessObject JavaScript database wrapper covered in Chapter 7. By having a simplified API, it enables programmers who are not familiar with AJAX to send and retrieve remote data without such a steep learning curve. If you know the API for one of these access objects, you know how to use the other one.

The constructor for the ServerAccessObject is the simplest of all its methods. The behavior is to store the URL of the remote server and then set and define the object's methods. The only functional line in the constructor, as shown in the following code, stores the URL for later use in the URL attribute of the object.

```
this.URL = URL;
```

This URL attribute is never accessed directly by the programmer. Programmers and engineers should also consider the `makeCall` method private in addition to the URL attribute.

The `makeCall` method is the heart and soul of the ServerAccessObject. It does all the work when the object is asked to perform any sort of server access. It is fronted by the two façade methods `getData` and `setData`. The API description in Table 8.2 describes their basic uses.

As you can see in the following section, one of the many standard methodologies of assigning methods to objects is used for these façades. This methodology creates a function object through the use of the `function` constructor call and assigns the result to an attribute of the current object represented by the `this` key word.

The two façade methods `getData` and `setData` are almost identical. They receive four parameters and then pass them plus three more to the underlying `makeCall` method. The additional parameters are the first, fifth, and seventh in the `getData` call and the first, third, and seventh in the `setData` call. The fifth parameter of the `makeCall` method is the data to be passed to the server as part of a POST type request. This is obviously not needed for the `getData` method, and therefore, null is passed.

```
this.getData = function(dataType, refresh,
                        parameterSequence, HTTPHeaders){

    var passThroughParameters =
```

```
                    generatePassThroughParameters();
        this.makeCall('GET', dataType, refresh,
                    parameterSequence, null, HTTPHeaders,
                    passThroughParameters);
    }
    this.setData = function(dataType, parameterSequence,
                                    data, HTTPHeaders){
        var passThroughParameters =
                    generatePassThroughParameters();
        this.makeCall('POST', dataType, true,
                    parameterSequence, data, HTTPHeaders,
                    passThroughParameters);
    }
```

The `generatePassThroughParameters` function call assembles all the information required to enable the framework to continue processing the BCFs and VCFs, mapped to the BCF using the ServerAccessObject. For more information on this function found in the QCUtilities.js file, see Chapter 5, "Hybrid Applications, GPS, Acceleration, and Other Native Functions with PhoneGap."

Table 8.2 **The Private makeCall Method API**

Attribute/Method	Return	Description	Parameters
makeCall(callType, dataType, refresh, parameterSequence, data, HTTPHeaders, passThroughParameters)	Void	A method that should be considered private. This method makes the actual AJAX calls to the server and handles the result.	callType—Either GET or POST. dataType—Either TEXT or XML. refresh—A Boolean flag indicating whether a refresh of the data should be enforced. parameterSequence—A string containing the URL parameters that are used in the request. data—Character or binary data sent with the request. Used with POST requests. HTTPHeaders—An associative array of HTTP Request header names and values. passThroughParameters—An array of values needed by the framework to continue processing after the data has been received from the server.

The third parameter of the `makeCall` method is a Boolean flag indicating whether the caching behavior of the client, in this case the UIWebView, should be active or inactive. In the case of the `setData` method, it is obvious that caching is a very bad behavior, so it is hard coded to `true` to turn off this caching.

By including these parameters in the method signature of `makeCAll`, it can now effectively encapsulate the behavior required for both retrieving and sending data to a remote server. This façade helper function pattern is often used, as in this case, when most but not all of the code for two or more methods/functions is the same and significant code duplication would occur if façades were not used.

To understand the `makeCall` method, you must understand the underlying JavaScript XMLHttpRequest object's API. This API is implemented in the UIWebView used in hybrid applications and Mobile Safari.

The only object in this API is the XMLHttpRequest object (see Table 8.3).

Table 8.3 **The XMLHttpRequest Object API**

Attribute/Method	Return	Description	Parameters
XMLHttpRequest()	XMLHttp Request	A constructor for the object.	None
abort()	void	Terminates the request of which it is a method.	None
getAllResponse Headers()	String	A string containing all of the response header names and values is returned as a result of this call.	None
getResponseHeader (aHeaderName)	String	Returns a string containing the value of the header with the given name or null if no such header exists.	AHeaderName—The name of the HTTP Response header for which you want the associated value.

Table 8.3 **The XMLHttpRequest Object API**

Attribute/Method	Return	Description	Parameters
open(type, URL, asynch, userName, passWord)	void	Opens and prepares a connection to the desired server.	type—A string of value GET or POST. Asynch—A Boolean flag indicating if the request should be made asynchronously. This should always be passed true. userName—An optional parameter that is the user name to gain access to the file or directory specified in the URL. password—An optional parameter that is the password for the specified user name to gain access to the file or directory specified in the URL.
send(data)	void	A method used to attach character or binary data to a request. This is used with POST type requests such as uploading files.	Data—The information attached to the request.
SetRequestHeader (name, value)	void	A method that can overwrite standard header values or add custom header names and values to a request.	Name—A string that is the identifier key of the header. Value—A string that is the value associated with the name.
onreadystatechange		An attribute that is set to be a function. The function set is called when the onreadystatechange event is fired. This happens each time the readyState changes.	

Table 8.3 **The XMLHttpRequest Object API**

Attribute/Method	Return	Description	Parameters
readyState		A series of integers that represents the state of the request that is made. The possible values are 0—The send method has not been called. 1—The request is being sent to the server. 2—The request has been received by the server. 3—A portion of the response has been received from the server. 4—A complete response has been received from the	
responseText		The data sent from the server as text minus any HTTP Response headers.	
responseXML		The data sent from the server as an XML DOM. If the data is not valid XML, this value is null.	
status		A number sent by the server indicating the success or failure state of a request: 404—not found and 200—success are the two of the most common. For a complete list, see http://www.w3.org/Protocols/rfc2616/rfc2616-sec10.html.	

Table 8.3 **The XMLHttpRequest Object API**

Attribute/Method	Return	Description	Parameters
statusText		A server-generated string containing any message that matches the status code.	

The commonly used methods of this API are the constructor, open, and send methods. A simple example of using these methods and other commonly used attributes is shown in the following code. It consists of requesting the main page of the open source WebKit project as text.

Notice two items in this simple example. The first is that the `request` object is global in scope. It is available for use in the `handleResponse` function that is called automatically by the browser engine when the `readyState` changes. This makes the code simple, but is a large problem if two requests need to be or are accidentally sent during overlapping times.

```
var request = new XMLHttpRequest();
request.onreadystatechange = handleResponse;
request.open('GET','http://webkit.org/', true);
request.sent('');

function handleResponse(){
    if(request.readyState == 4){
        if(request.status == 200){
            var result = response.responseText;
            //do something with the result.
        }
    }
}
```

Because of the global scope of this `request` variable, this simple example is not thread-safe. Because these requests are asynchronous, it is possible and often likely that requests will clobber each other. The ServerAccessObject encapsulates this global variable to solve this problem.

The second item to note is that the request is being sent to a full URL. In standard browsers, an XMLHttpRequest object can request data only from the server that it originated from. The UIWebView in hybrid applications does not have this restriction. It can request data from any server because it is not a browser, which is both a boon and a bane.

The reason for the restriction in browsers is to stop cross-site scripting, XSS, attacks. These can occur if malicious JavaScript is inserted into otherwise innocent HTML that your application has requested. Because the UIWebView is not a browser, you are now responsible for defending the application against such attacks. Thankfully, the QuickConnectiPhone framework supplies you with the ability to map Security Control Functions (SCF), and the ServerAccessObject calls them before passing the results of the requests to your VCFs.

These SCFs are created like VCFs and are mapped using the `mapCommandToSCF` function. See Section 4 for an example of creating and using SCFs.

The XMLHttpRequest object API contains no indicator for forcing a refresh. The ServerAccessObject handles this by setting one of the standard HTTP Request headers.

```
if(refresh){
    /*
    *   if we are to disable caching and force a call to the server, then the 'If-
Modified-Since' header will
    *     need to be set to some time in the past.
    */
    http.setRequestHeader( "If-Modified-Since", "Sat, 1 Jan 2000 00:00:00 GMT" );
}
```

The `If-Modified-Since` header tells the server that it should send data if the requested item has a modified date after the date included in the header value. By setting the value to a date and time in the past, it guarantees that cached data is not used.

On the other hand, the ServerAccessObject API has no flag enabling the user to define the request as synchronous or asynchronous. It is well accepted that all AJAX calls should be asynchronous. This keeps the web engine responsive to further input from the user. If they are synchronous, when the user rotates the iPhone, the UIWebView would become a blank, white screen. This also happens if the user decides to scroll the view while a request is made to the server, which would yield a bad user experience. Because it is such a bad idea to use the XMLHttpRequest object synchronously, the ServerAccessObject hardcodes all requests to be asynchronous.

Unlike the earlier simple example, the ServerAccessObject does not use a standalone function to handle the `onreadystatechange` events. Instead, it uses an anonymous function (see Chapter 3, "Creating iPhone User Interfaces," for information regarding anonymous functions). The choice of using an anonymous function was made because of the capability of such functions to exist in the scope of the overlying function.

In this case, all local variables declared in the `makeCall` method are also available in the `onreadystatechange` anonymous function. Thus, the global variable problem discussed earlier is solved. By declaring a variable, `http`, to be the newly created XMLHttp RequestObject to be used in the `makeCall` method, it automatically is still in scope when the `onreadystatechange` anonymous function is called.

For those new to the idea of anonymous functions, this seems counterintuitive. For those who are used to them, it might seem as if you are getting away with something you shouldn't be able to do. The following code contains this entire anonymous function.

```
http.onreadystatechange = function(){

   if(http.readyState == ServerAccessObject.COMPLETE){
       //the standard holder for all types of data queries
       var queryResult = new QueryResult();
      //these are custom error headers that you can
      //send from your server code if you choose.
      queryResult.errorNumber =
                        http.getResponseHeader('QC-Error-Number');
       queryResult.errorMessage =
                         http.getResponseHeader('QC-Error-Message');
       if(http.status != ServerAccessObject.HTTP_OK
                 && http.status != ServerAccessObject.HTTP_LOCAL
                 && http.status !=
                         ServerAccessObject.OSX_HTTP_File_Access){

              queryResult.errorNumber = http.status;
              queryResult.errorMessage = "Bad access type.";
       }

             /*
              *  Retrieve the data if the server returns that the
       *  processing of the request was successful or if
 *  the request was directly for a file on
 *  the server disk.
              *  Get it as either Text or XML
              */
       if(queryResult.errorNumber == null){
            queryResult.data = http['response'+dataType];
            if(!dispatchToSCF(passThroughParameters[0],
                                        queryResult.data)){
                queryResult.errorNumber =
                  ServerAccessObject.INSECURE_DATA_RECEIVED;
                         queryResult.errorMessage =
                            "Insecure data recieved.";
            }
      }
      /*
   *  Call the next Control Function in the
   *  list passing the resultData
       */
    if(window.callFunc){
         /*
  *  This may have been called from outside
```

```
45  *  a dispatchToBCF function.
46 *  If so, then there has been no callFunc
47 *  function defined.
48           */
49           var theResults = new Array();
50           theResults.push(queryResult);
51           theResults.push(passThroughParameters);
52           requestHandler(passThroughParameters[0],
53                 passThroughParameters[2], theResults);
54       }
55   }
56
57 };
```

Lines 30 to 36 in the previous code segment contain the SCF and VCF calls mentioned previously. Line 30 looks like the code in the front controller found in Chapter 2. In fact, it is nearly identical to the `checkValidation` function call described and behaves the same way.

Just as a user can type in bad data, a server can send bad data. The `checkSecurity` function is an application controller type function just like `checkValidation`. It calls any SCFs you have mapped in the mapping.js `file` to the same command that is mapped to the BCF using the ServerAccessObject. This way, you can apply any number of security checks to data received from a server, which helps you solve the problem with cross-site scripting attacks.

After checking the data, it is then added to a QueryResults object so that your application can continue to process it. This is done by a call to the `requestHandler` function. The `passThroughParameters` are used here because they contain the command that triggered the call to your BCF, and the control function should be called next. By calling `requestHandler`, the ServerAccessObject's `makeCall` method ensures that all of your control functions are called in the order you mapped them in the mappings.js file. Because the result object, `theResults`, is also passed, it is made available to all of the subsequent control functions. This means that you can then use the data in any way you see fit.

Because the `onreadystatechange` anonymous function contains these two application controller type function calls and because it is the only function to which a server sends data, it acts as an additional front controller for your application. This means that if you use the ServerAccessObject for all your remote data access, you gain the advantages for all of the remote communications that were discussed in Chapter 2 for standard applications.

The double-front controller pattern provides the needed security in your applications and yet enables you the flexibility of retrieving data from any server. Figure 8.3 shows how both of these front controllers protect your application and your data.

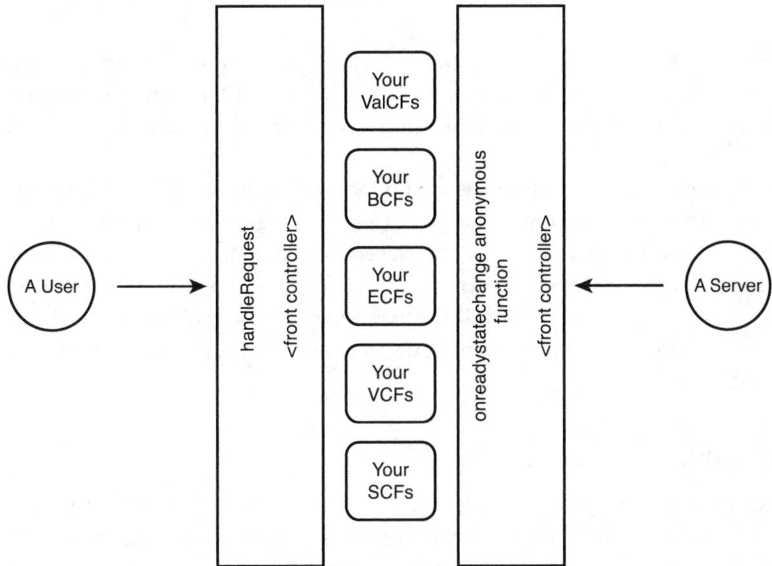

Figure 8.3 Both users and servers can provide bad data to an application. The double-front controller pattern protects your application code from faulty and possibly nefarious data.

Section 4: Security Control Functions

SCF are called by the ServerAccessObject to ensure the validity and safety of the data retrieved from a server. They act in much the same way and role as ValCFs covered in Chapter 2. They also follow the same pattern as all the other control functions.

For a SCF to be called, it must be mapped to a command. For example, your application might require a user to log in for it to send back JSON type data on success. An example of such a mapping is

```
mapCommandToSCF('login',  checkForFunctions);
```

This means that you would also need to have a `checkForFunctions` function that can be called by `checkSecurity`.

Because of the json2 library available in the QciPhone/json2.js file, this function becomes easy to write.

```
Function checkForFunctions(data){
      if(data == JSON.stringify(JSON.parse(data){
             return true;
      }
      return false;
}
```

When the data is parsed, the `JSON.parse` method puts additional characters into the string if it encounters function declarations or function calls. This causes these attempts to define or make function calls to fail, providing much needed security from cross-site scripting, XSS, attacks.

Your check can then take advantage of this by turning the newly created JavaScript object back into a string and comparing it against the original. If it fails the comparison test, the application knows that the data retrieved from the server contains malicious code.

This means that JSON text sent to you cannot contain function definitions or function calls. This is actually very good. If this were not so, you could never tell if the JavaScript functions in the JSON were your code or malicious code inserted in the middle XSS attack.

Summary

The ServerAccessObject provides you with an easy, secure way to retrieve data from remote sources into your hybrid application. It provides you with an easy-to-use API that is similar to the DataAccess API to reduce your learning curve.

With the addition of SCFs, the code you retrieve can be as thoroughly checked as you deem fit.

The ServerAccessObject can retrieve remote data and store it for later use via the DataAccessObject or use it directly as the browserAJAXExample application does. It also opens up the possibility of synchronizing data stored on the local machine with data stored on a remote machine.

The ServerAccessObject enables you to create code that can automatically notify a web server should the application code fail. You can also use it to collect metrics from your iPhone application and send them to a server to help make the application faster and easier to use.

All of this is now available easily on your installed hybrid iPhone application due to the ServerAccessObject.

Appendix A
Introduction to JSON

JavaScript Object Notation (JSON) is an interesting creation. It enables you to convert JavaScript objects and arrays into strings that can be passed over a network or stored in a database. Later, these strings can be reconstituted on another computer or after database retrieval. This capability to serialize and inflate JavaScript objects and arrays opens up possibilities. This appendix shows you an Application Programmer Interface (API) for a well-accepted JavaScript JSON library and gives you simple examples that show the library in action.

Section 1: Background

Passing information from one system to another is always a problem. This is especially evident in web application development where a server can be written in almost anything and run on many different types of computers. XML was one of the early device-, OS-, and language-agnostic formats proposed to solve this problem, and it has some good uses. Using XML for some data transfers is overkill, especially the small pieces of information generally sent using AJAX. XML becomes wordy if all you want to send is a small array of numbers or a key/value map. This problem was solved not by the invention of new technology but by utilizing a capability already built into interpreted languages.

All major loosely typed interpreted languages have an `eval` type of functionality that executes strings as if they are source code. This `eval` functionality is a powerful and dangerous capability. If it is misused, it can completely open an application to hacking and abuse. In addition, all major loosely typed interpreted languages have the capability to define arrays and objects without a call to an instantiation keyword similar to `new`.

If you look at JavaScript examples, you can easily see how to create an array. The first example is an object-oriented approach:

```
var array = new Array();
array.push(5);
array.push(13);
array.push('hello');
```

A second example is a nonobject-oriented approach:

```
var array = [5,13,'hello'];
```

Both of these examples create identical arrays. The second example is the one that is interesting to a discussion of JSON. It, coupled with the capability of JavaScript to evaluate a string as if it is code, makes JSON possible.

The following code creates a string of characters that matches how a programmer would use the second example to create an array. It is not the array itself, but a description of what the array should be.

```
var someString = "[5,13,'hello']";
//evaluate the string
var array = eval(someString);
```

The last line of the previous example parses the string into JavaScript source code, interprets the JavaScript, and executes it. In this simple example, the string is in the same application as the `eval` call, and therefore, the process is silly. If, however, the string came from the Objective-C side of a QuickConnectiPhone application, or, as is done traditionally from a server, the `eval` call makes much more sense.

The production of objects is similar. The object-oriented approach, shown here, creates an object and then adds attributes to it:

```
var object = new Object();
object.width = 5;
object.height = 13;
object.message = 'hello';
```

The corresponding nonobject-oriented approach is

```
var object = {"width":5,"height":13,"message":"hello"};
```

The following is the JSON-like code:

```
var someString = '{"width":5,"height":13,"message":"hello"}';
//evaluate the string
var object = eval(someString);
```

Although this is the heart of JSON, implementing it on your own is dangerous. For example, if the string had been passed from JavaScript to the Objective-C side of QuickConnectiPhone and somehow the string includes complex instructions, it could possibly delete everything on your hard drive.

JSON libraries have already been created to handle this security problem for you. The one used on the JavaScript side is Json2 and is found in the json2.js file. Json2 is one of the most commonly used JavaScript JSON parsers. Because you regularly pass and receive data to and from the Objective-C side of QuickConnectiPhone-based applications, you need to understand the API for this library.

Section 2: A JSON JavaScript API

The Json2 API, found in Table A.1, is simple and straightforward. It consists of only two functions: one to turn an object or an array into a string and another to turn strings into objects. The first is called `stringify`.

Table A.1 **The Json2 API**

Function	Parameters
`JSON.stringify(entity, replacer, space, linebreak)`	**Required Parameters:** **entity**—The JavaScript object, array, or primitive to be converted. **Optional Parameters:** **replacer**—A function or array that enables you to override the default string generation for values associated with the JavaScript entities' keys. **space**—A number or character such as '\t' or that is used to indent JavaScript entities that are values stored with keys in other entities. **linebreak**—A character or characters that overrides the default '\n' such as '\r\n' or .
`JSON.parse(string, reviver)`	**Required Parameters:** **String** —The JSON string to be converted into a JavaScript object or array. **Optional Parameters:** **Reviver**—A function with the inverse behavior of a replacer used in the `stringify` method.

The `stringify` function has several parameters, but for QuickConnectiPhone, you need only the first one. It is an object or array to be converted to a string. A generic example is as follows:

```
var JSONString = JSON.stringify(object);
```

The conversion of strings into objects is just as simple:

```
var object = JSON.parse(someString);
```

Arrays are handled in exactly the same fashion.

A complete example, object_JSON_example.html, of using Json2 to stringify and parse objects can be found in the Examples/JSON directory of the QuickConnectiPhone download. Figure A.1 shows the result of converting an object into a string, converting it back to an object, and then printing the `size` attribute of the object.

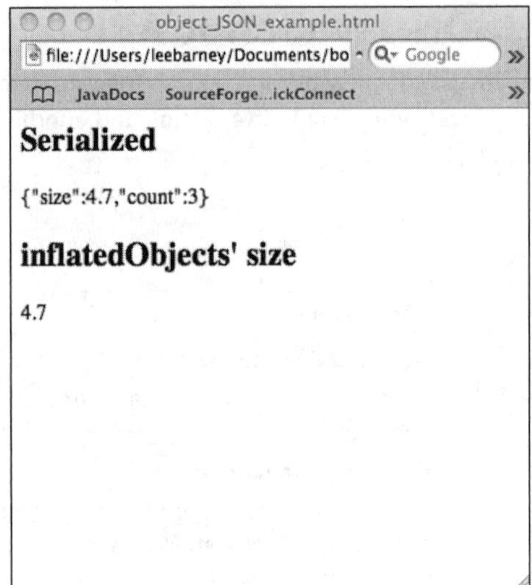

Figure A.1 The result of stringifying and then parsing an object

An example also exists in the Examples/JSON directory and is called array_JSON_example.html. It illustrates how to use Json2 to stringify and parse with arrays. Figure A.2 shows an example.

Notice that both of these examples use the industry standard words serialize and inflate for the results of the `stringify` and `parse` functions, respectively.

The Json2 library also enables you to pass primitives such as numbers. String objects are also handled well. This is not true of all JSON libraries in all languages. Figure A.3 shows the example being run.

Using the Json2 library, you can pass anything to stringify and parse and it will be handled correctly. The JSON library on the Objective-C side also correctly handles primitives and strings.

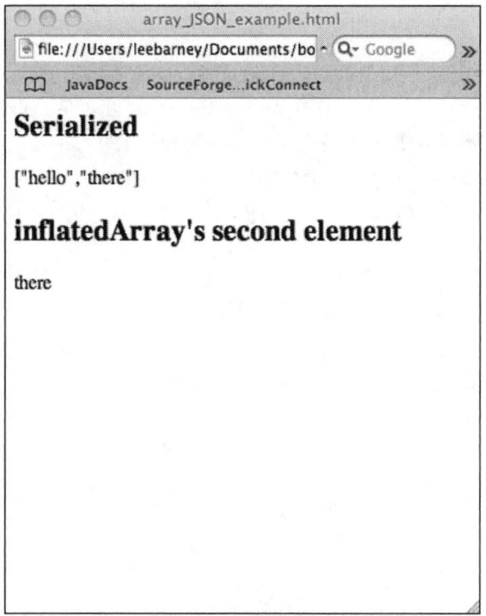

Figure A.2 The result of stringifying and then parsing an array

Figure A.3 The result of stringifying and then parsing primitives and strings

Summary

JSON is a wonderful way to pass information. It is device-, operating system-, and language-agnostic. There are free, open source parsers in all the commonly used languages, and some of them (such as PHP) ship with them.

The Json2 library included with QuickConnectiPhone is easy to use and enables you to send data to and receive data from the Objective-C side of the hybrid application.

Appendix B

The QuickConnectFamily Development Roadmap

Because QuickConnectiPhone is early in its development cycle, it is rapidly undergoing change. As such, it is important to closely watch the development for updates. Table B.1 shows what is available for download as of February 23, 2009.

Yes indicates that the functionality is shipping. *In Development* indicates that work is actively being done on the feature. *Development Planned* means that the feature is possible but not yet in development. *Not Possible* means that the feature is not available on the device. Dashed cells indicate that work is not being done at the time of writing this book.

Note

Although development is planned for Windows and Windows Mobile, because no development is being done at this time, Table B.1 does not list them.

Table B.1 **The QuickConnectFamily Development Roadmap on February 23, 2009**

	iPhone	Android	Mac	Linux	Symbian
Geolocation	Yes	Yes	Not Possible	Not Possible	—
Accelerometer	Yes	Yes	In Development	—	—
Vibration	Yes	Yes	Not Possible	Not Possible	—
Ad-hoc networking	Yes	In Development	In Development	In Development	In Development
JavaScript Database wrapper (SQLite)	Yes	Not Possible	Yes	In Development	In Development
Installed Native Database wrapper (SQLite)	Yes	Yes	Yes	Yes	In Development

Table B.1 **The QuickConnectFamily Development Roadmap on February 23, 2009**

	iPhone	Android	Mac	Linux	Symbian
AJAX wrapper	Yes	In Development	Yes	Yes	In Development
Drag and Drop Library	Yes	—	Yes	Development Planned	—
Synch cable networking	In Development	—	—	—	—
Camera access	In Development	In Development	In Development	—	—
Image Geolocation	In Development	—	—	—	—
System Sounds (Play)	Yes	Yes	Yes	In Development	In Development
Record/Play audio files	Yes	Yes	In Development	Development Planned	Development Planned
Native Date/Time pickers	Yes	—	—	—	—
Embedded Google maps	Yes	In Development	—	—	—
Charting and graphing	Yes	—	Yes	—	—

Definitions:

Geolocation—Getting current GPS location coordinate data.

Accelerometer—Getting the x, y, and z directional changes.

Vibration—Causes the device to vibrate.

Ad-hoc networking—Finding and communicating with other devices nearby running the same application.

JavaScript Database wrapper (SQLite)—Using the built-in HTML 5 database.

Native Database wrapper (SQLite)—Using SQLite databases shipped with an application.

AJAX wrapper—An easy-to-use AJAX library to retrieve remote data.

Drag and Drop Library—An easy-to-use library to enable the user to move, spin, and resize screen items.

Synch cable networking—Accessing and transferring data to your desktop machine using the synch cable.

Camera access—Taking and storing pictures.

Image Geolocation—Accessing the geolocation information embedded in picures taken with the device.

System Sounds (Play)—Playing short (less than 5 seconds) sounds.

Record/Play audio files—Recording audio using the device and playing those files and audio files shipped as part of your application.

Native Date/Time pickers—Displaying and using the Objective-C based pickers rather than the limited JavaScript ones.

Embedded Google maps—Custom Google maps in your application rather than standard ones, or displaying the map application.

Charting and graphing—An easy-to-use charting library for displaying line, bar, pie, and other charts.

Appendix C

The PhoneGap Development Roadmap

Because PhoneGap is early in its development cycle, it is rapidly undergoing change. As such, it is important to closely watch the development for updates. Table C.1 is from the PhoneGap wiki. It shows what developers claim about the availability of functions and what has been confirmed as of the time of writing this book.

Confirmed means JavaScript functions are found in PhoneGap as of February 23, 2009. The author is unable to comment on the availability of the Blackberry platform. *In Work* means that the PhoneGap team is working to make this feature available. *Claimed* means that the PhoneGap team states that the feature is available, but the author cannot find evidence of this in the downloaded code. Dashed cells indicate that work is not being done and does not currently exist. *Not Possible* indicates that the developers believe that the functionality indicated is not accessible on the device.

Note

Development for Symbian and Windows Mobile is planned, but no work has been done; therefore, they are not in Table C.1.

Table C.1 **PhoneGap Development Roadmap on February 23, 2009**

	iPhone	Android	Blackberry (OS 4.5)
Geolocation	Confirmed	Confirmed	Claimed
Accelerometer	Confirmed	Confirmed	Available in OS 4.7
Camera	In Work	In Work	In Work
Vibration	Confirmed	Confirmed	Claimed
Offline (local files)	In Work	Claimed	In Work
Contacts API	Claimed	—	Claimed
SQLite wrapper	Claimed	—	Not Possible

Table C.1 **PhoneGap Development Roadmap on February 23, 2009**

	iPhone	Android	Blackberry (OS 4.5)
XMPP API	—	—	—
File system IO	—	In Work	In Work
Gesture / Multitouch	Confirmed as part of basic UIWebView	—	—
SMS API	—	In Work	—
Telephone API	In Work	In Work	In Work
Copy / Paste	Not Possible	—	Claimed
System Sounds (Play)	Confirmed	—	—
Sounds (Record)	—	—	—
Bluetooth	—	—	—
Wifi ad-hoc connection	—	—	—
Maps	Claimed	In Work	In Work
Orientation change	Confirmed	—	—
Network availability	—	—	—

Definitions:

Geolocation—Getting GPS location coordinate data.

Accelerometer—Getting x, y, and z directional changes.

Camera—Taking and storing pictures.

Vibration—Causes the device to vibrate.

Offline (local files)—Installed HTML, CSS, and JavaScript files (they are not on a web server).

Contacts API—Access to the information in the contacts application.

XMPP API—Jabber-like messaging.

File system IO—Reading and writing to flat text or binary files.

Gesture/Multi-touch—Using one or more fingers for complex data input.

SMS API—Instant messaging.

Telephone API—Placing phone calls.

Copy / Paste—Duplication of input.

System Sound (Play)—Playing audio files.

Sounds (Record)—Recording audio using the device.

Bluetooth—Using Bluetooth connectivity to other devices.

Wifi ad-hoc connection—Finding and communicating with other devices.

Maps—Using Google maps.

Orientation change—Detecting portrait and landscape device changes.

Network availability—Detecting if the device has network access.

Index

A

abort method, 164

accel command, 78

accelerometers, PhoneGap, 109

access. *See* **database access; remote data access**

ADC (Apple Developer Connection), 8

add function, 29

alert behavior, PhoneGap, 99

Alert dialog, hybrid applications and, 2

anonymous functions, 136

APIs, Json2 API, 175-176

Apple Developer Connection. *See* **ADC (Apple Developer Connection)**

application controllers, 32

applicationDidFinishLaunching method, 16, 19

applications

- BrowserAJAXAccess sample application, 155-157
- BrowserDBAccess sample application, 127
- hybrid applications, Alert dialog and, 2
- immersion applications, 55-57
- nonlist-based view applications, 51-55

arrays

- converting to strings, 175
- creating, 173-174
- passThroughParameters, 137
- retVal, 153

asynchronous, 39

AudioServicesPlaySystemSound function, 103

B

BCFs (Business Control Functions), 26, 29, 32-33, 39
Browser part, 48-50
BrowserAJAXAccess sample application, 155-157
BrowserDBAccess sample application, 127
business application controllers, 38-41
Business Control Functions (BCF), 26

C

calculateSolutionsBCF, 30
callback method, 106
callFunc function, 41
changeView function, 49
checkNumbersValCF function, 32
checkSecurity function, 170
classes
  DataAccessObject
    methods, 129-130
    with native SQLLite databases, 133-134
    with WebKit engine databases, 135-145
    with WebView SQLLite databases, 130-133
  GlassAppDelegate, 17
  QuickConnectViewController, 17
  singleton classes, 89
  SQLiteDataAccess, 145-154
code attribute (SQLError), 142
control functions, 28
converting objects/strings, 175
copying files, 6
CSS transforms, creating custom, 57-63
cube transition, 54
custom PhoneGap template, 9-11

D

Dashcode, 1
  directories, 7
  QuickConnectiPhone template, 1-3
  transitions, 52-54
data, retrieving, 26
DataAccessObject class
  methods, 129-130
  with native SQLLite databases, 133-134
  with WebKit engine databases, 135
    Database object, 137-139
    dbAccess method, 137
    generatePassThroughParameters function, 137
    getData method, 136
    passThroughParameters array, 137
    sample code listing, 143-145
    setData method, 136
    SQLError object, 141-142
    SQLResultSetRowList object, 140-141
    SQLResultSet object, 140
    SQLTransaction object, 139-140
  with WebView SQLLite databases, 130-133
DataAccessObject method, 129
DataAccessObject.js file, 129
database access
  BrowserDBAccess sample application, 127
  database terminology, 128
  native databases, 145-154
    getDeviceData method, 145-146
    getNativeData method, 145
    makeCall function, 146
    SendDBResultVCO object, 153
    setNativeData method, 145

SQLite3 API, 147-150
native SQLite databases, 133-134
overview, 127
WebKit engine databases, 135
Database object, 137-139
dbAccess method, 137
generatePassThroughParameters function, 137
getData method, 136
passThroughParameters array, 137
sample code listing, 143-145
setData method, 136
SQLError object, 141-142
SQLResultSetRowList object, 140-141
SQLResultSet object, 140
SQLTransaction object, 139-140
WebView SQLite databases, 129-133

Database object, 137-139

dbAccess method, 137, 142

delegates, 14

deleteScoreBCF function, 133

development roadmaps
for PhoneGap, 183-185
for QuickConnectiPhone, 179-181

development tools
PhoneGap, 183-185
QuickConnectiPhone, 179-181

device activation
JavaScript, 75-81, 95-102
Objective-C, 81-88, 102-109

Device.exec function, 99

Device.init method, 96

Device.Location.init method, 100

Device.Location.set method, 106

Device.vibrate method, 98

didAccelerate method, 109

didUpdateToLocation method, 109

directories, Dashcode, 7

dispatchToBCF function, 38-39

dispatchToECF function, 43

dispatchToValCF function, 35

dispatchToVCF function, 41-42

displaying
maps from within QuickConnect JavaScript applications, 111-115
pickers, 80

displayScoresVCF View Control Function, 131, 134

displaySiteDataVCF function, 159-161

displaySolutionVCF function, 30

dissolve transitions, 53

doCommand method, 86, 92, 116, 153

DollarStash game, 56

done method, 61

double underscore (__), 97

drag and drop, 46
hopping elements, 59
modules, 64-74

drag-and-drop scale rotation API, 64

dragAndGesture example, 65

E

ECF (Error Control Functions), 30, 33, 42-43

embedding
Google Maps, 111-115
web content
PhoneGap, 23-24
QuickConnectiPhone, 19-23

entryECF function, 30

error application controllers, 42-43

eval function, 33

eval type, 173

executeSQL method, 139, 143

F

fade transitions, 54
fields (database), 128
files
  copying, 6
  DataAccessObject.js, 129
  ServerAccessObject.js, 159
flip transitions, 54
foreign keys, 128
frameworks, 25-26
FrontController API, 28
functions. *See also specific functions*
  anonymous functions, 136
  SCF (security control functions), 171-172
future developments
  for PhoneGap, 183-185
  for QuickConnectiPhone, 179-181

G

__gap_device_model variable, 97
__gap variable, 97
generatePassThroughParameters function, 137
GestureEvent, 62
gestures, 46, 62
getAllResponseHeaders method, 164
getData method, 129, 131, 136, 158, 162-163
getDeviceData method, 145-146
getGPSLocation function, 79
getInstance method, 89
getNativeData method, 130, 134, 145
getResponseHeader method, 164
getSiteDataBCF function, 159
GlassAppDelegate class, 17
goForward method, 50
Google Maps, displaying within QuickConnect JavaScript applications, 111-115
goSub function, 52
gotAcceleration function, 101
GPS
  JavaScript, 79-80
  Objective-C, 86-87
  PhoneGap, 99-101, 105-106
groups, Xcode, 7

H

handleRequest function, 28, 34
handleRequestCompletionFromNative method, 154
HIG (Human Interface Guide), 45-47
HistoryExample application, 48
hopping elements, 59
hybrid applications, Alert dialog and, 2

I

immersion applications, 55-57
InfoWindow, 115, 126
initWithContentsOfFile method, 107
initWithFrame method, 116
insertID attribute (SQLResultSet), 140
instantiating objects, 12
interfaces
  CSS transforms, 57-63
  list-based interfaces, 48-50
  view-based applications, 49-51
  views, 50
isDraggable, 66
item method, 141

J-K-L

JavaScript
- device activation, 75-81, 95-102
- modularity, 25-34
- scroll function, 119

JSON (JavaScript Object Notation), 78, 161
- Json2 API, 175-176
- Objective-C device activation, 83
- overview, 173-174

Json2 API, 175-176

JSONStringify method, 153

L

length attribute (SQLResultSetRowList), 141

list-based interfaces, 48-50

loadView method, 20

M

makeCall function, 75-77, 146, 162-164

makeChangeable function, 64, 67

makeDraggable function, 64-66

mapCommands method, 84

mapCommandToCo method, 93

mapping function API, 30

maps
- displaying from within QuickConnect JavaScript applications, 111-115
- QuickConnect mapping module, implementing with Objective-C, 115-126
- zooming, 122-125

MapView, 115

math command, 28-31

medical imaging applications, 55

message attribute (SQLError), 142

methods. *See* ***specific methods***

modularity
- control functions, 28
- JavaScript, 25-26
  - implementing in QuickConnectiPhone, 34-38
  - QuickConnect JavaScript framework example, 26-34

modules
- defined, 25
- drag-and-drop, 64-74
- rotation, 67-74
- scaling, 67-74

moveX:andY method, 124

N

native databases, accessing, 145-154
- getDeviceData method, 145-146
- getNativeData method, 145
- makeCall function, 146
- SendDBResultVCO object, 153
- setNativeData method, 145
- SQLite databases, 133-134
- SQLite3 API, 147-150

nonlist-based view applications, 51-55

NSLog function, 93

O

Objective-C, 11-14
- device activation, 81-88, 102-109
- implementing QuickConnectiPhone architecture, 88-94
- implementing QuickConnect mapping module, 115-126
- instantiating objects, 12
- PhoneGap application structure, 17-19
- pickers, 88
- QuickConnectiPhone application structure, 14-17

objects. *See also specific objects*
converting strings to, 175
converting to strings, 175
creating, 174
instantiating with Objective-C, 12
oldScale attribute, 67
ongesturechange event, 71
onreadystatechange anonymous function, 168-170
onreadystatechange attribute, 165
ontouchchange listener, 59
ontouchend listener, 61
open method, 165
openDatabase method, 138

P

parse function, 175
passThroughParameters array, 137
pathForResource:ofType method, 21
PhoneGap, 1-3, 97-98
accelerometers, 109
alert behavior, 99
custom PhoneGap templates, Xcode, 9-11
development roadmap, 183-185
embedding web content, 23-24
GPS, 99-101, 105-106
JavaScript device activation, 95-102
notifying the user that something has gone wrong, 99
Objective-C application structure, 17-19
Objective-C device activation, 102-109
system sound, 107-108
versus QuickConnectiPhone, 9
pickers
displaying, 80
Objective-C, 88
Pin, 115, 120
pinch, 46
play command, 77
playing
recordings, 78
system sounds, 85
playSound method, 76, 101
playTweetSound function, 101
pointers, 12
prepared statements, 132-133
prepareDrag function, 67
prepareGesture function, 71
primary keys, 128
principal-delegate relationships, 14
principals, 14
protocols, 15
provisioning, 8
proxies, 14
push transitions, 53

Q

QCCommandObjects, 92
QuickConnect JavaScript framework
displaying maps from, 111-115
modularity example, 26-34
QuickConnect mapping module, implementing with Objective-C, 115-126
QuickConnectFamily installer, 1
QuickConnectiPhone
development roadmap, 179-181
embedding web content, 19-23
implementing modular design, 34-38
Objective-C application structure, 14-17

Objective-C implementation, 88-94
versus PhoneGap, 9
QuickConnectiPhone templates
Dashcode, 1-3
Xcode, 4-8
QuickConnectViewController class, 17

R

rangeOfString method, 104
readyState method, 166
recordings
playing, 78
stopping, 79
records, 128
recursion, 41
remote data access
BrowserAJAXAccess sample application, 155-157
overview, 155
SCF (security control functions), 171-172
ServerAccessObject, 157
displaySiteDataVCF function, 159-161
getData method, 158, 162-163
getSiteDataBCF function, 159
makeCall method, 162-164
onreadystatechange anonymous function, 168-170
ServerAccessObject method, 158
setData method, 158, 162-163
XMLHttpRequest object, 164-167
requestHandler function, 170
responseText method, 166
responseXML method, 166
retrieving data, 26
retVal array, 153
revolve transition, 54
rotate functions, 63
rotation, 67-74
rows attribute (SQLResultSet), 140
rowsAffected attribute (SQLResultSet), 140

S

scaling modules, 67-74
SCF (security control functions), 171-172
scroll function, 119
security control functions (SCF), 171-172
send method, 165
SendDBResultVCO object, 153
sendloc command, 87
ServerAccessObject, 157
displaySiteDataVCF function, 159-161
getData method, 158, 162-163
getSiteDataBCF function, 159
makeCall method, 162-164
onreadystatechange anonymous function, 168-170
ServerAccessObject method, 158
setData method, 158, 162-163
XMLHttpRequest object, 164-167
ServerAccessObject method, 158
ServerAccessObject.js file, 159
setData method, 129-132, 136, 158, 162-163
setMapLatLngFrameWithDescription method, 125
setNativeData method, 130, 145
SetRequestHeadert method, 165
setStartLocation function, 59
shouldStartLoadWithRequest function, 82
showDateSelector function, 80
showMap function, 114
showPickResults command, 80

SimpleExampleAppDelegate method, 19
singleton classes, 89
singleTouch message, 120
slide transitions, 53
SQLError object, 141-142
SQLite databases, accessing
native SQLite databases, 133-134
WebKit engine databases, 135
Database object, 137-139
dbAccess method, 137
generatePassThroughParameters function, 137
getData method, 136
passThroughParameters array, 137
sample code listing, 143-145
setData method, 136
SQLError object, 141-142
SQLResultSetRowList object, 140-141
SQLResultSet object, 140
SQLTransaction object, 139-140
WebView SQLite databases, 129-133
SQLite3 API, 147-150
sqlite3_bind_blob method, 149
sqlite3_bind_double method, 150
sqlite3_bind_int method, 150
sqlite3_changes method, 148
sqlite3_close method, 147
sqlite3_column_blob method, 149
sqlite3_column_bytes method, 149
sqlite3_column_count method, 148
sqlite3_column_double method, 148
sqlite3_column_int method, 148
sqlite3_column_name method, 148
sqlite3_column_text method, 149
sqlite3_column_type method, 148
sqlite3_errmsg method, 147
sqlite3_finalize method, 149
sqlite3 object, 147
sqlite3_open method, 147
sqlite3_prepare_v2 method, 148
sqlite3_step method, 148
sqlite3_stmt method, 147
SQLiteDataAccess class, 145-154
SQLResultSetRowList object, 140-141
SQLResultSet object, 140
SQLTransaction object, 139-140
standard behaviors, 46
statements, prepared, 132-133
status messages (XMLHttpRequest), 166
statusText string (XMLHttpRequest), 165-167
stopping playing of recordings, 79
stringByEvaluatingJavaScriptFromString method, 154
stringify function, 175
strings, converting, 175
subviews, 21
Subviews list, 49
swap transition, 54
swipe, 46
switches, 47
synchronous, 39
system sounds
JavaScript, 76-77
PhoneGap, 107-108
playing with Objective-C, 85

T

tables, 128
templates
custom PhoneGap template, 9-11
Dashcode, 1-3
QuickConnectiPhone, 4-8

terminatePlaying function, 79
textual user input, 47
Touch class, 58
touch events, 58
touch locations, 46
touchable images, 51
touchesBegan method, 122
touchesMoved:withEvent method, 118, 124
transaction method, 138, 142
transforms (CSS), 57-63
transitions, 52-55
translate function, 61
translation, 72
types, eval, 173

U

UIWebView API, 21
UIWebView class, 19-20
updating user viewable screens, 26
user input, validating, 26
user viewable screens, updating, 26

V

ValCF, 29, 33, 38
ValCF (Validation Control Functions), 26
validating user input, 26
VCF (View Control Functions), 26, 29, 33, 38, 42
vibrations, 76, 82, 98-99, 103-104
view application controllers, 38-39, 41-42
view-based applications, 49-51
views, 50

W

web content, embedding
  with PhoneGap, 23-24
  with QuickConnectiPhone, 19-23
WebKit engine databases, accessing, 135
  Database object, 137-139
  dbAccess method, 137
  generatePassThroughParameters function, 137
  getData method, 136
  passThroughParameters array, 137
  sample code listing, 143-145
  setData method, 136
  SQLError object, 141-142
  SQLResultSetRowList object, 140-141
  SQLResultSet object, 140
  SQLTransaction object, 139-140
webKitTransform, 58-60
webMapView, 117
webView:shouldStartLoadWithRequest: navigationType function, 103
WebView SQLite databases, accessing, 129-133
webViewDidStartLoad method, 102

X-Y-Z

Xcode
  custom PhoneGap template, 9-11
  groups, 7
  QuickConnect templates, 4-8
XMLHttpRequest method, 164
XMLHttpRequest object, 164-167

zooming maps, 122-125

Your purchase of **Developing Hybrid Applications for the iPhone** includes access to a free online edition for 45 days through the Safari Books Online subscription service. Nearly every Addison-Wesley Professional book is available online through Safari Books Online, along with more than 5,000 other technical books and videos from publishers such as Cisco Press, Exam Cram, IBM Press, O'Reilly, Prentice Hall, Que, and Sams.

SAFARI BOOKS ONLINE allows you to search for a specific answer, cut and paste code, download chapters, and stay current with emerging technologies.

Activate your FREE Online Edition at www.informit.com/safarifree

STEP 1: Enter the coupon code: QDVUNCB.

STEP 2: New Safari users, complete the brief registration form.
Safari subscribers, just log in.

If you have difficulty registering on Safari or accessing the online edition, please e-mail customer-service@safaribooksonline.com

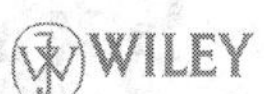